PIANO · VOCAL · GUITAR

THE BEST GOSPEL SONGS EVER

ISBN 0-634-00602-9

HAL•LEONARD®
CORPORATION
7777 W. BLUEMOUND RD. P.O. BOX 13819 MILWAUKEE, WI 53213

Visit Hal Leonard Online at
www.halleonard.com

GOSPEL

SONGS

AMAZING GRACE

Words by JOHN NEWTON
Traditional American Melody

taught my heart to fear, and grace my fears re - lieved.
prom - ised good to me, His word my hope se - cures.

How pre - cious did that grace ap - pear the
He will my shield and por - tion be as

hour I first be - lieved. 2. Through
long as life en - dures.

Verse 3
And when this flesh and heart shall fail
and mortal life shall cease.
I shall possess within the veil
a life of joy and peace.

When we've been there ten thousand years,
bright shining as the sun.

We've no less days to sing God's praise
than when we first begun.

AT CALVARY

Words by WILLIAM NEWELL
Music by D.B. TOWNER

1. Years I spent in van-i-ty and pride,
2.-4. *(See additional lyrics)*

Car - ing not my Lord was cru-ci-fied, Know - ing not it was for me He died On Cal - va - ry.

Additional Lyrics

2. By God's Word at last my sin I learned;
   Then I trembled at the law I'd spurned,
   Till my guilty soul imploring turned To Calvary.
   REFRAIN

3. Now I've giv'n to Jesus ev'rything,
   Now I gladly own Him as my King,
   Now my raptured soul can only sing Of Calvary.
   REFRAIN

4. Oh, the love that drew salvation's plan!
   Oh, the grace that bro't it down to man!
   Oh, the mighty gulf that God did span At Calvary.
   REFRAIN

AT THE CROSS

Text by ISAAC WATTS
Music by RALPH E. HUDSON

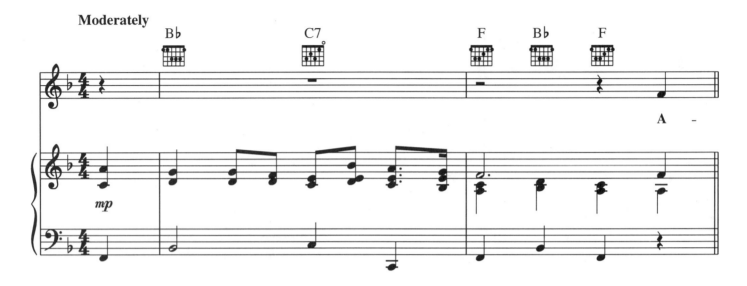

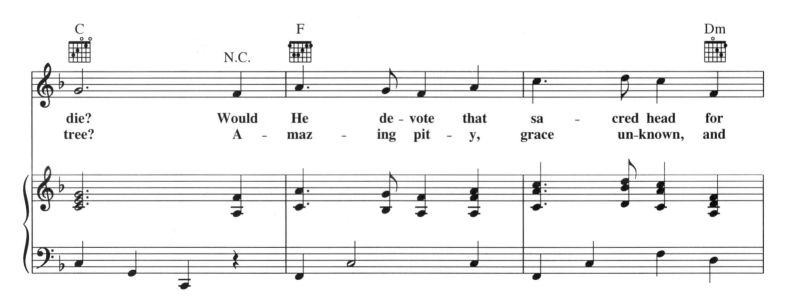

A -

las, and did my Sav - ior bleed and did my Sov - 'reign
it for crimes that I have done and He groaned up - on the

die? Would He de - vote that sa - cred head for
tree? A - maz - ing pit - y, grace un - known, and

BECAUSE HE LIVES

Words by WILLIAM J. and GLORIA GAITHER
Music by WILLIAM J. GAITHER

12

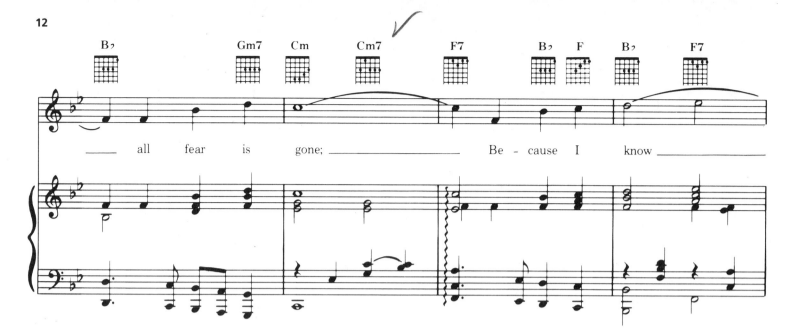

____ all fear is gone; _____ Be - cause I know _____

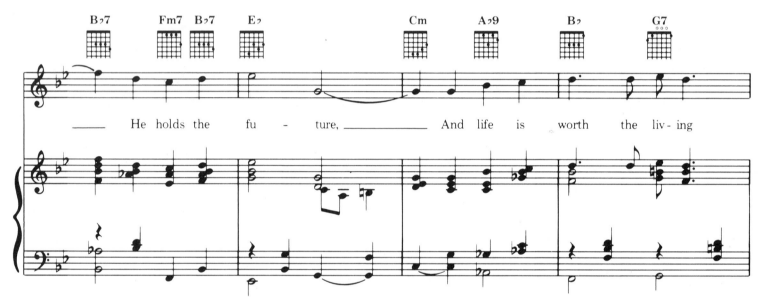

____ He holds the fu - ture, _____ And life is worth the liv - ing

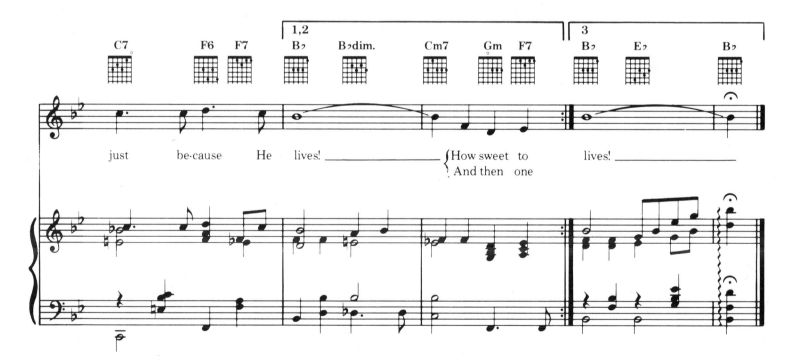

just be-cause He lives! _____ { How sweet to _____ lives! _____
{ And then one

3. And then one day I'll cross that river;
   I'll fight life's final war with pain;
   And then as death gives way to vict'ry,
   I'll see the lights of glory and I'll know He reigns.

BEHOLD THE LAMB

Words and Music by
DOTTIE RAMBO

14

BLESSED ASSURANCE

Lyrics by FANNY CROSBY and VAN ALSTYNE
Music by PHOEBE P. KNAPP

With movement

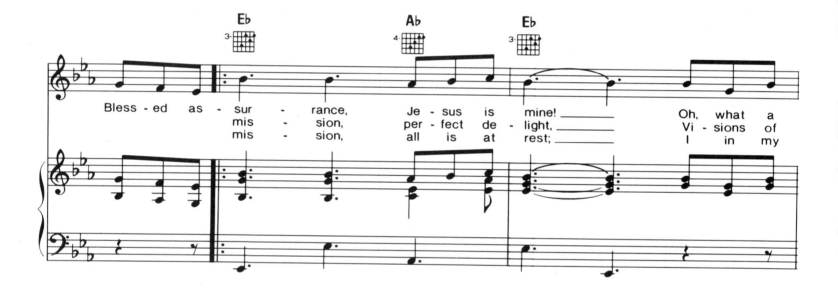

Bless-ed as - sur - rance, Je - sus is mine! _____ Oh, what a
mis - sion, per - fect de - light, _____ Vi - sions of
mis - sion, all is at rest; _____ I in my

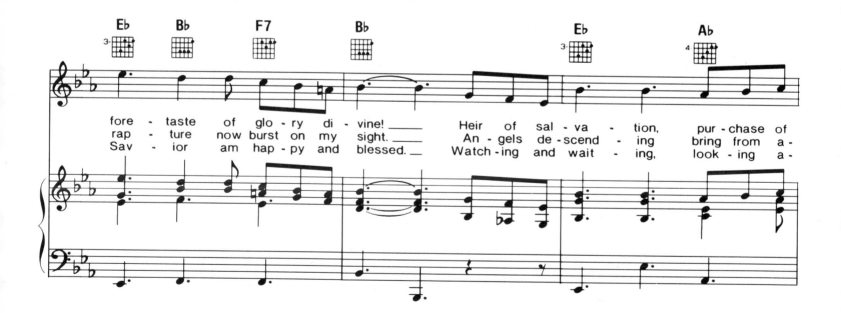

fore - taste of glo - ry di - vine! _____ Heir of sal - va - tion, pur - chase of
rap - ture now burst on my sight. _____ An - gels de - scend - ing bring from a -
Sav - ior am hap - py and blessed. __ Watch - ing and wait - ing, look - ing a -

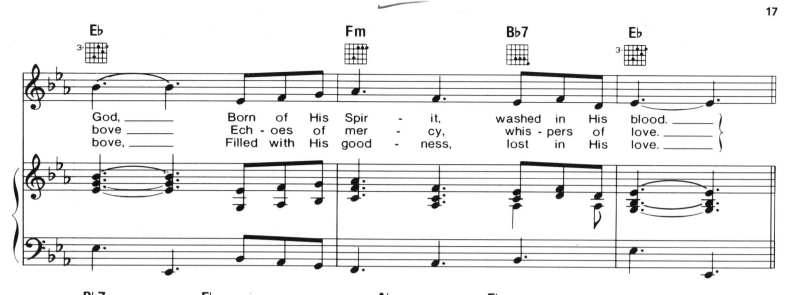

God, _____ Born of His Spir - it, washed in His blood. _____
bove _____ Ech - oes of mer - cy, whis - pers of love. _____
bove, _____ Filled with His good - ness, lost in His love. _____

This is my sto - ry, this is my song, _____ Prais - ing my

Sav - ior all the day long. _____ This is my sto - ry this is my

song, ___ Prais - ing my Sav - ior all the day long. ___ Per - fect sub -
Per - fect sub - long. _____

CAN HE, COULD HE, WOULD HE, DID HE?

Words and Music by DWIGHT LILES
and JOHN CHISUM

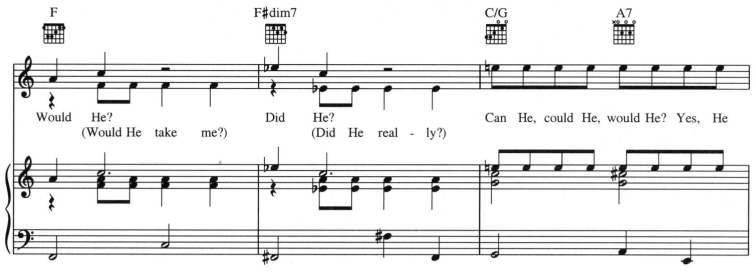

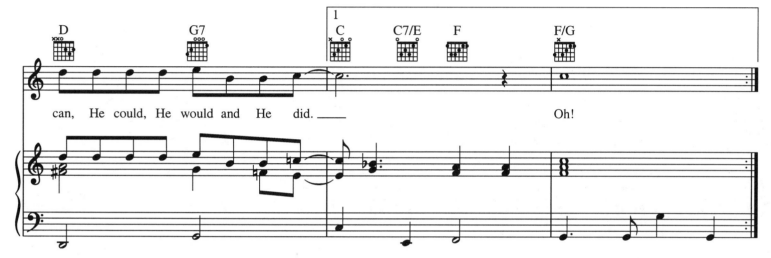

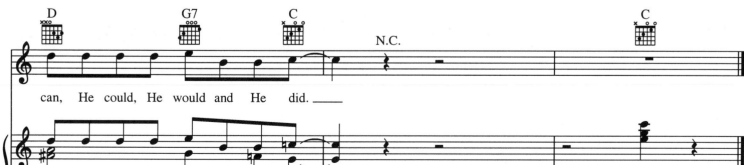

DADDY SANG BASS

Words and Music by
CARL PERKINS

Moderately fast

I re-mem-ber when I was a lad, times were hard and things were bad; But there's a

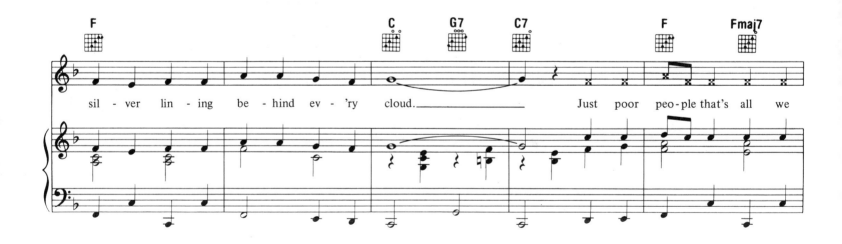

sil-ver lin-ing be-hind ev-'ry cloud._____ Just poor peo-ple that's all we

were,___ try-in' to make a liv-in' out of black and dirt; We'd get to-geth-er in a fam-ily

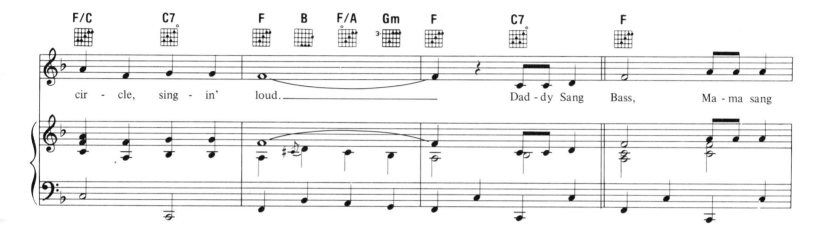

cir-cle, sing-in' loud._____ Dad-dy Sang Bass, Ma-ma sang

ten-or me and lit-tle bro-ther would join right in there Sing-in' seems to help a trou-bled

soul;_____ One of these days and it won't be long, I'll re-

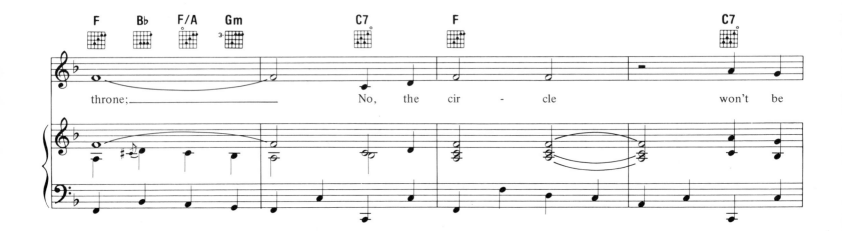

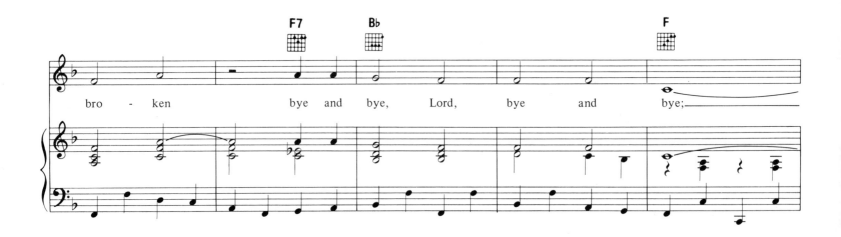

THE DAY HE WORE MY CROWN

Words and Music by
PHIL JOHNSON

DO LORD

Traditional

Moderately fast

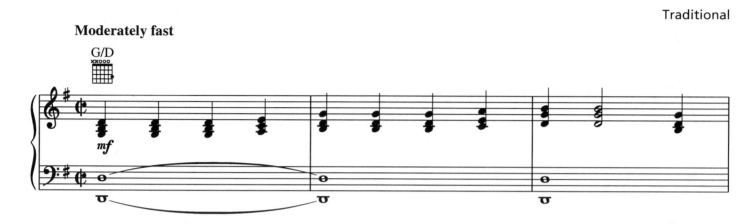

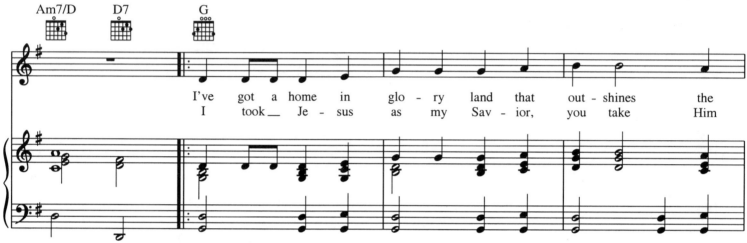

I've got a home in glo - ry land that out - shines the sun.
I took __ Je - sus as my Sav - ior, you take Him too.

sun. I've got a home in glo - ry land that
too. I took __ Je - sus as my Sav - ior,

out - shines the sun. I've got a home in glo - ry land that
you take Him too. I took __ Je - sus as my Sav - ior,

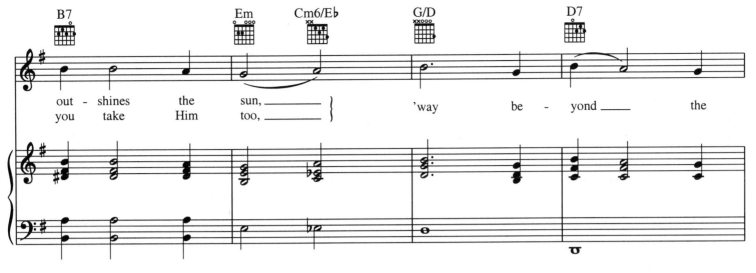

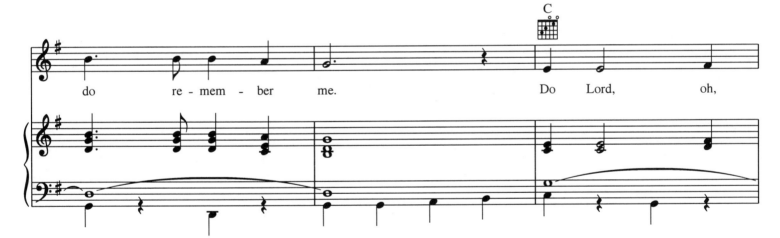

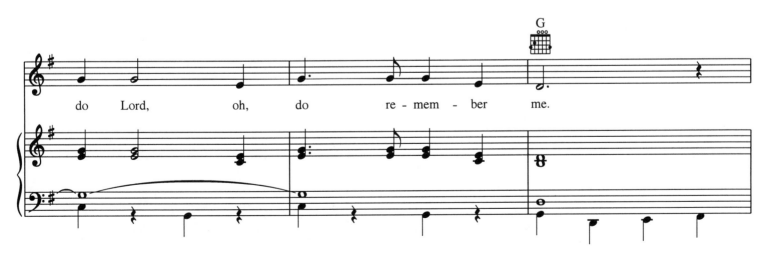

GET ALL EXCITED

Words and Music by
WILLIAM J. GAITHER

Get all ex - cit - ed, go tell ___ ev - 'ry-bod - y that Je - sus

Christ is King. ___ I said, get all ex - cit - ed, go tell ___ ev - 'ry-bod - y that

Je - sus Christ is King. ___ I said, get all ex - cit - ed, go tell ___

32

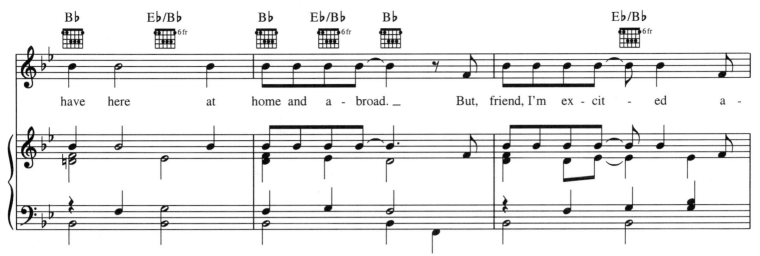

have here at home and a - broad. _ But, friend, I'm ex - cit - ed a -

bout a so - lu - tion for the world, I'm _ a - gon - na shout and sing, _ and it's

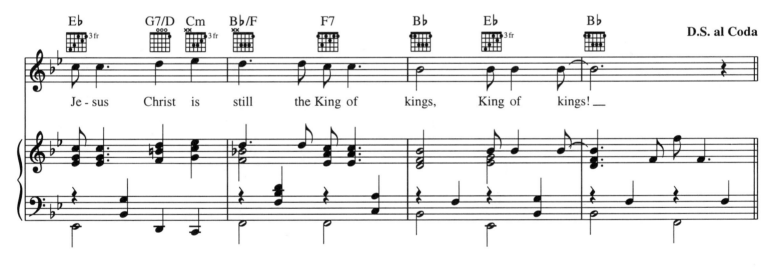

Je - sus Christ is still the King of kings, King of kings! _

D.S. al Coda

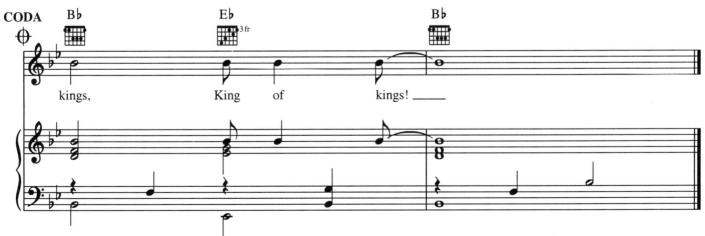

CODA

kings, King of kings! _____

THE FAMILY OF GOD

Words by WILLIAM J. and GLORIA GAITHER
Music by WILLIAM J. GAITHER

Verse

1. You will no-tice— we say bro-ther _____ and sis-ter _____ 'round here, It's be-
2. From the door of an orph-'nage— to the house of _____ the King, No—

cause we're a fam-'ly _____ and these folks are so near. When
long-er an out-cast,— a _____ new song I sing. From

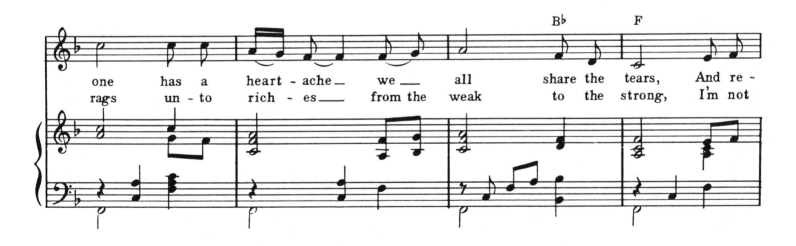

one has a heart-ache— we ___ all share the tears, And re-
rags un-to rich-es _____ from the weak to the strong, I'm not

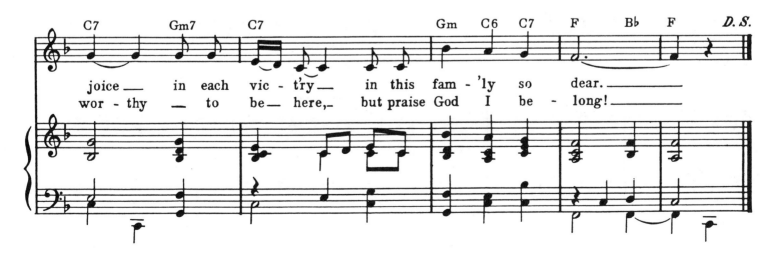

joice ___ in each vic-t'ry ___ in this fam-'ly so dear. _____
wor-thy ___ to be— here,— but praise God I be- long! _____

FILL MY CUP, LORD

Words and Music by
RICHARD BLANCHARD

Chorus

Fill my cup, Lord, _____ I lift it up, Lord, _____ Come and quench this thirst-ing of my

soul, Bread of Heav-en, Feed me till I want no more, Fill my

cup, Fill it up and make me whole.

There are
So, my whole. _____

3. So, my brother, if the things this world gave you
Leave hungers that won't pass away,
My blessed Lord will come and save you
If you kneel to Him and humbly pray.

GIVE ME THAT OLD TIME RELIGION

Traditional

Moderately bright

Chorus

Give Me That   Old Time Re - li - gion;   Give Me That   Old Time Re -

li - gion.   Give Me That   Old Time Re - li - gion and it's good e - nough for

Verse

me.   1. It was   good   for the Proph - et   Dan - iel;   it was
        2. It was   good   for Paul and   Si - las,   it was

Chorus

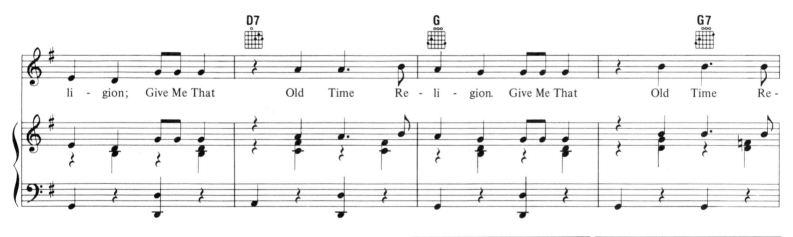

3. It was good for old Abe Lincoln;
It was good for old Abe Lincoln.
It was good for old Abe Lincoln,
And it's good enough for me.

GIVE THEM ALL TO JESUS

Words and Music by BOB BENSON SR.
and PHIL JOHNSON

Moderately

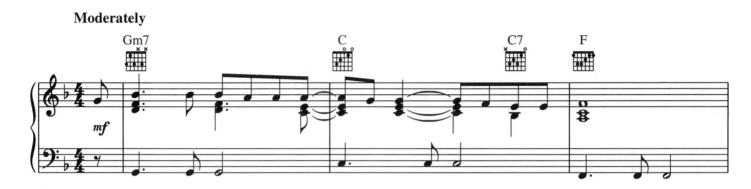

Are you tired of chas - in' _____ pret - ty rain -
He nev - er said _____ you'd on - ly see sun -

- bows? _____
- shine, _____

And are you tired of spin -
And He _____ nev - er said _____

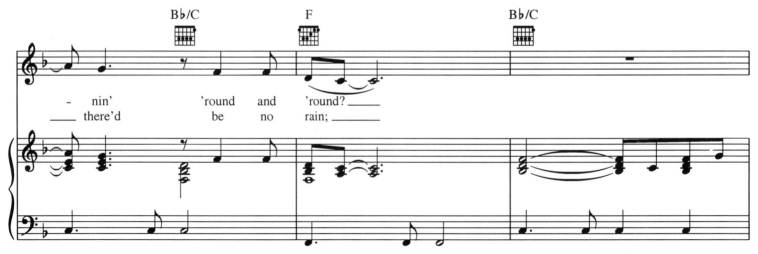

- nin' _____ 'round and 'round? _____
_____ there'd be no rain; _____

Wrap up all the shat - tered dreams _____ of your _____ life, _____
He on - ly prom - ised a heart full of sing - in', _____

And at the feet of Je - sus lay them
A-bout the ver - y things _____ that once brought

down.
pain. }
Give them all, give them all, _____

give them all _____ to Je - sus: shat - tered dreams, wound - ed hearts _____

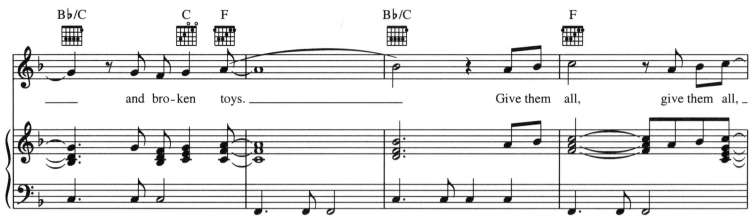

and bro-ken toys. _____ Give them all, give them all, _

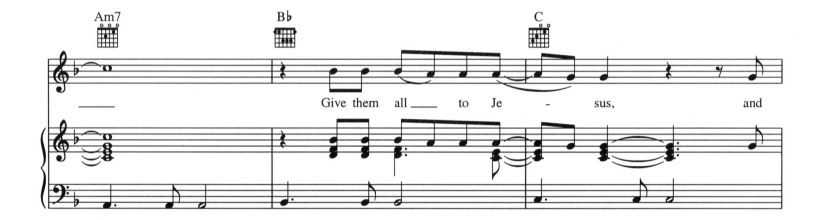

_____ Give them all ____ to Je - sus, and

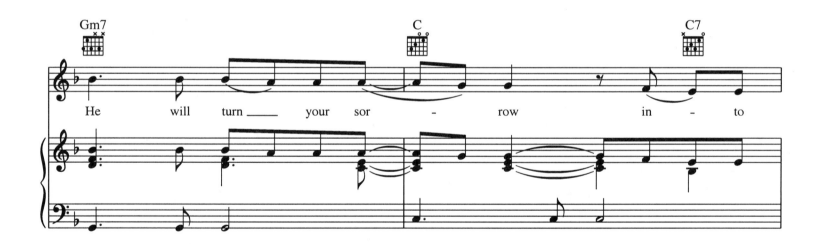

He will turn ____ your sor - row in - to

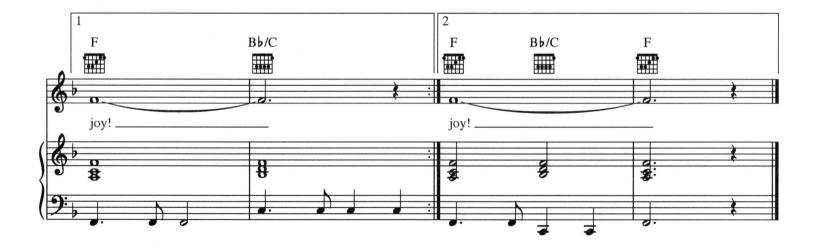

1.
joy! _____

2.
joy! _____

HE LOOKED BEYOND MY FAULT

Words and Music by
DOTTIE RAMBO

With expression

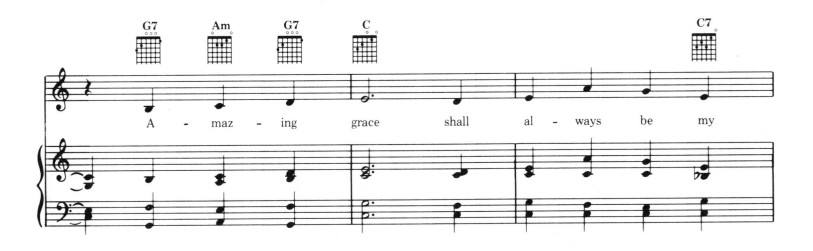

A - maz - ing grace shall al - ways be my

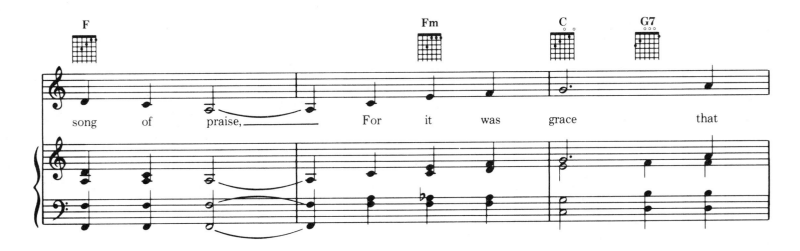

song of praise,_____ For it was grace that

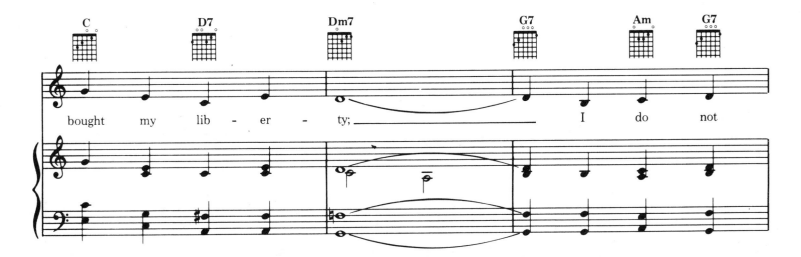

bought my lib - er - ty;_____ I do not

know just why He came to love me so, _____

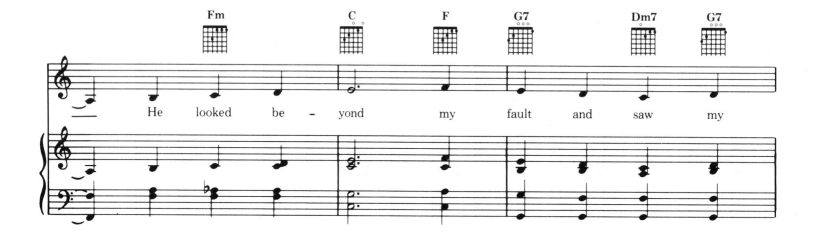

He looked be - yond my fault and saw my

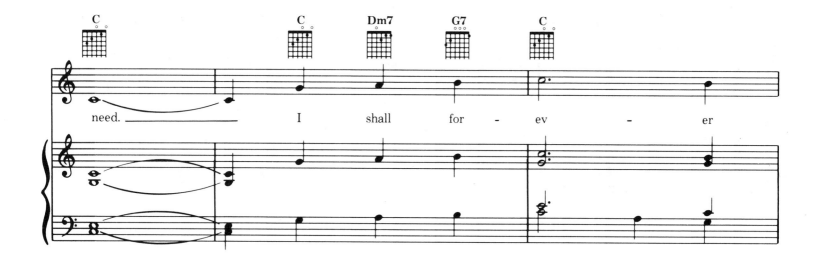

need. _____ I shall for - ev - er

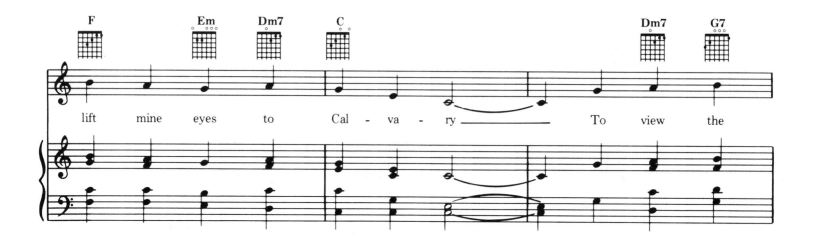

lift mine eyes to Cal - va - ry _____ To view the

45

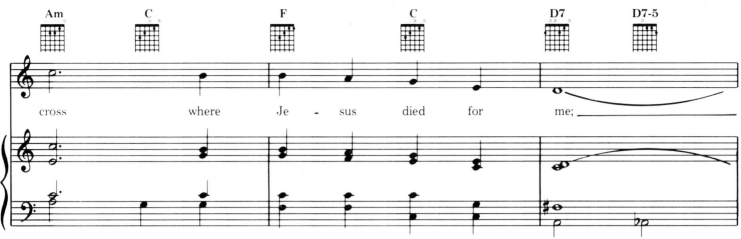

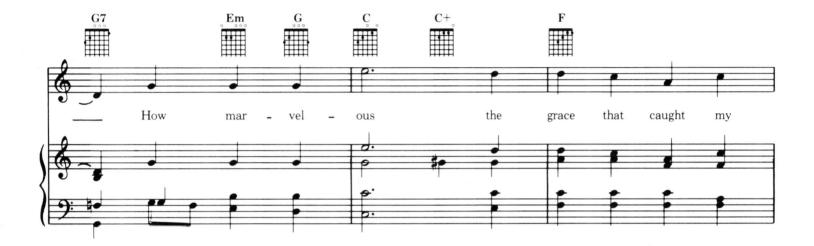

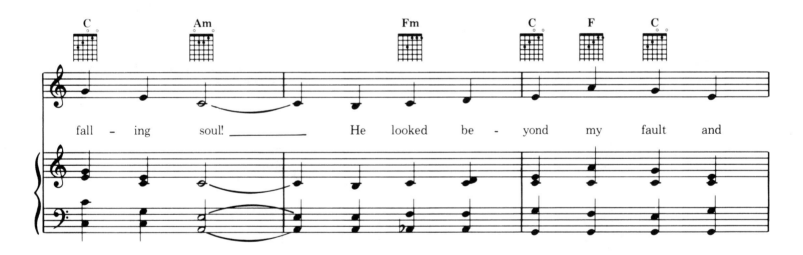

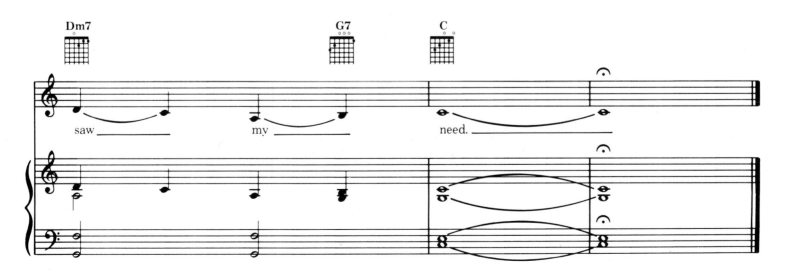

GOD SAID IT, I BELIEVE IT, THAT SETTLES IT!

Words and Music by STEPHEN R. ADAMS
and GENE BRAUN

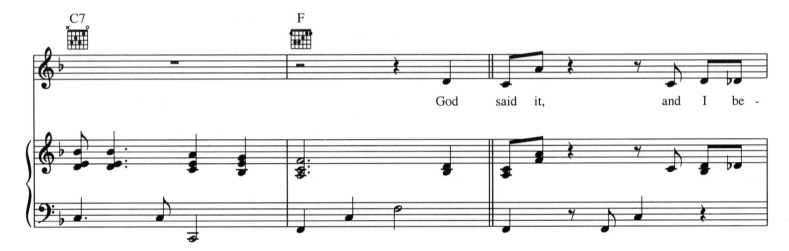

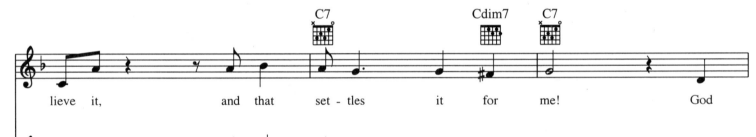

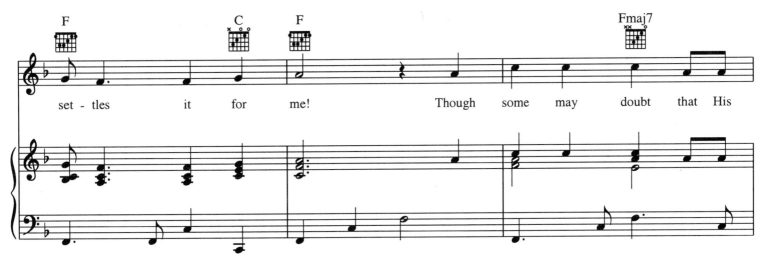

set-tles it for me! Though some may doubt that His

Word is true, I've cho-sen to be-lieve it; now

how a-bout you? God said it, and I be-

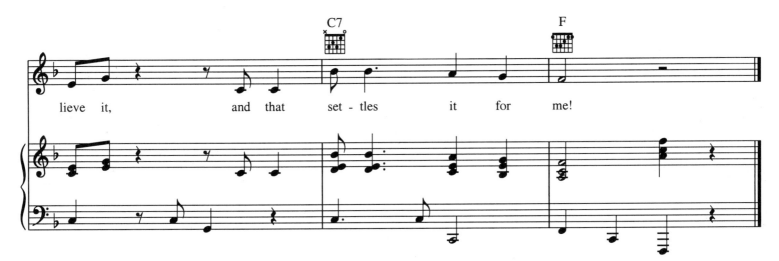

lieve it, and that set-tles it for me!

HALLELUJAH, WE SHALL RISE

By J.E. THOMAS

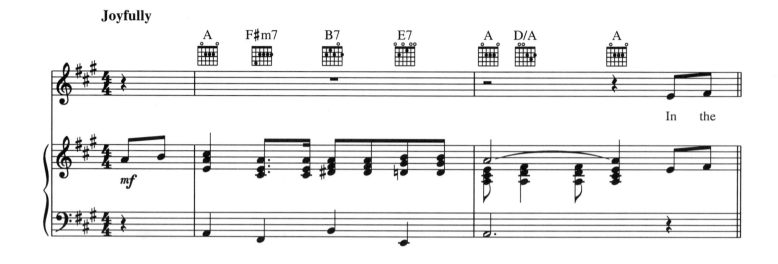

HE LOVED ME WITH A CROSS

Words and Music by JOEL LINDSEY
and SUE SMITH

HEAVEN CAME DOWN

Words and Music by
JOHN W. PETERSON

HE TOUCHED ME

Words and Music by
WILLIAM J. GAITHER

HE'S STILL WORKIN' ON ME

Words and Music by
JOEL HEMPHILL

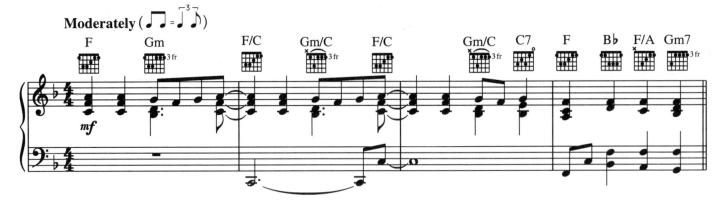

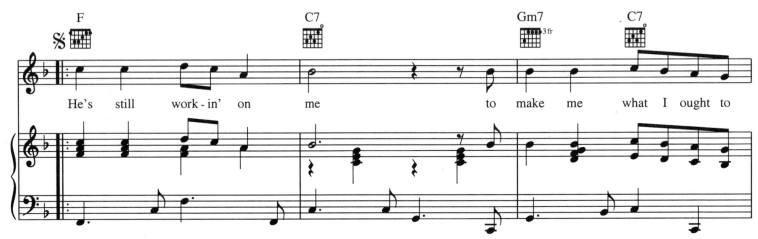

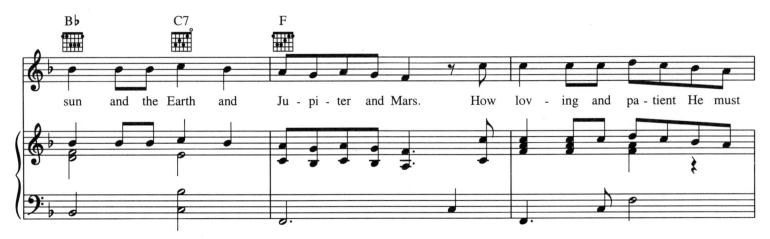

HIGHER GROUND

Words by JOHNSON OATMAN, JR.
Music by CHARLES H. GABRIEL

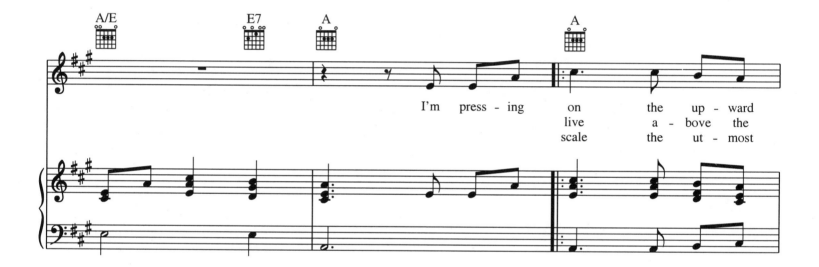

I'm press - ing on the up - ward
live a - bove the
scale the ut - most

way, new heights I'm gain - ing ev - 'ry day; still pray - ing
world, tho Sa - tan's darts at me are hurled; still for faith has
height, and catch a gleam of glo - ry bright; but still I'll

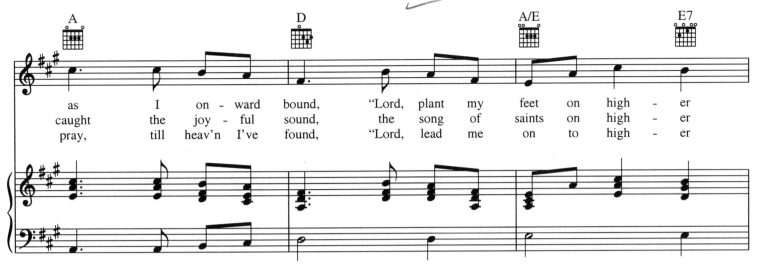

as   I   on - ward   bound,   "Lord,   plant   my   feet   on   high - er
caught   the   joy - ful   sound,   the   song   of   saints   on   high - er
pray,   till heav'n I've   found,   "Lord,   lead   me   on   to   high - er

ground."
ground. } Lord,   lift   me   up   and   let   me   stand,   by   faith,   on
ground."

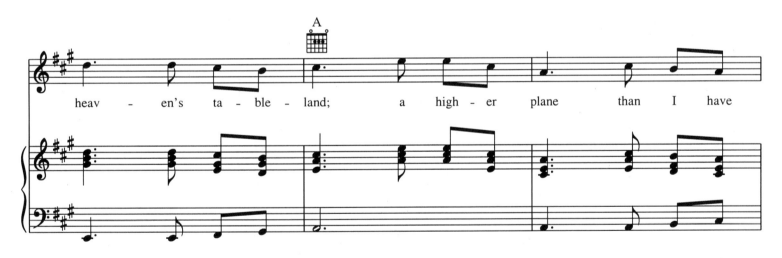

heav - en's ta - ble - land;   a   high - er   plane   than   I   have

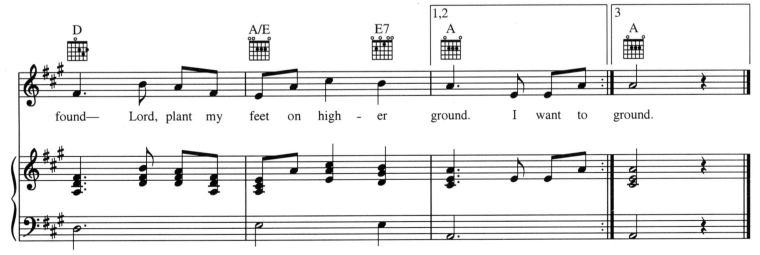

found— Lord, plant my feet on high - er ground. I want to ground.

HIS EYE IS ON THE SPARROW

Text by CIVILLA D. MARTIN
Music by CHARLES H. GABRIEL

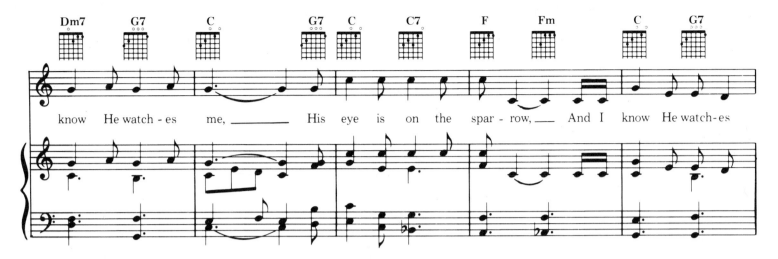

know He watch - es me, _____ His eye is on the spar - row, ___ And I know He watch-es

Chorus

me. ___ I sing be-cause I'm hap - py, _____ I sing be-cause I'm free; _____ For His

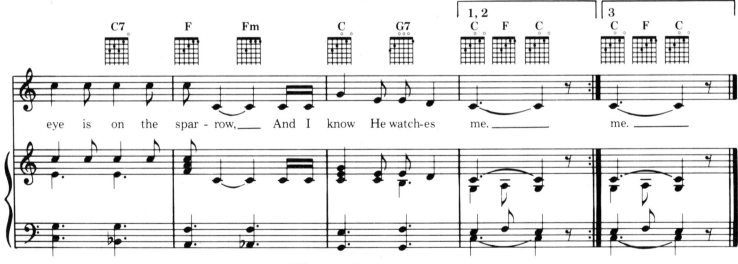

eye is on the spar - row, ___ And I know He watch-es me. _____ me. _____

3. Whenever I am tempted,
   Whenever clouds arise.
   When song gives place to sighing,
   When hope within me dies.
   I draw the closer to Him,
   From care He sets me free:

HIS NAME IS WONDERFUL

Words and Music by
AUDREY MIEIR

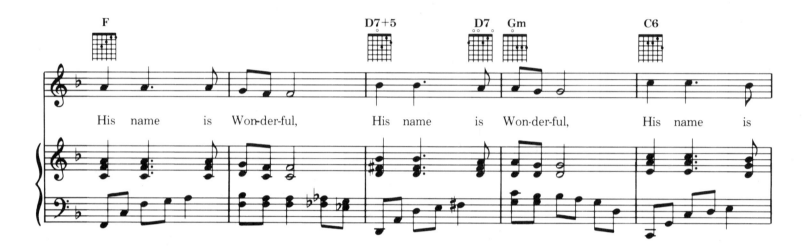

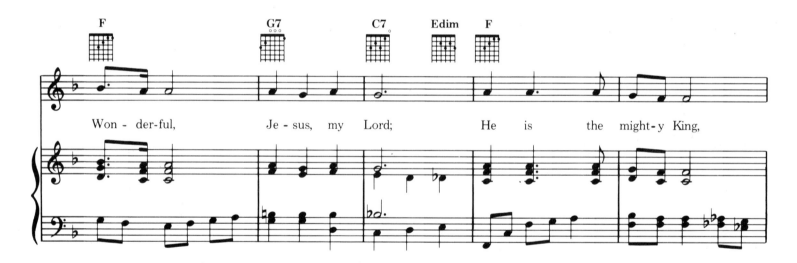

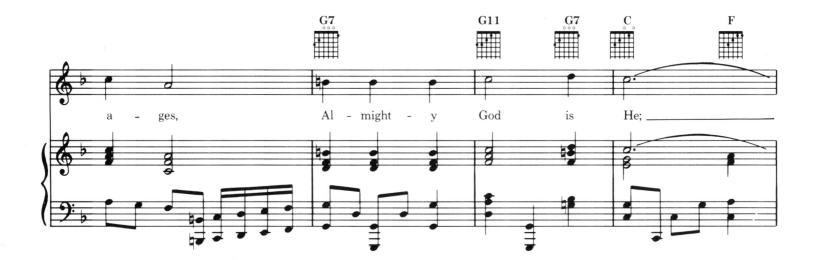

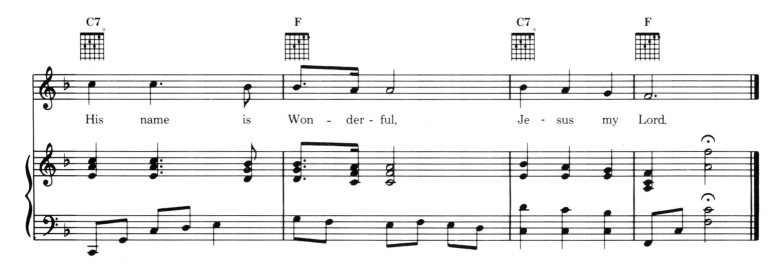

HOME WHERE I BELONG

Words and Music by
PAT TERRY

Easy four

1. They

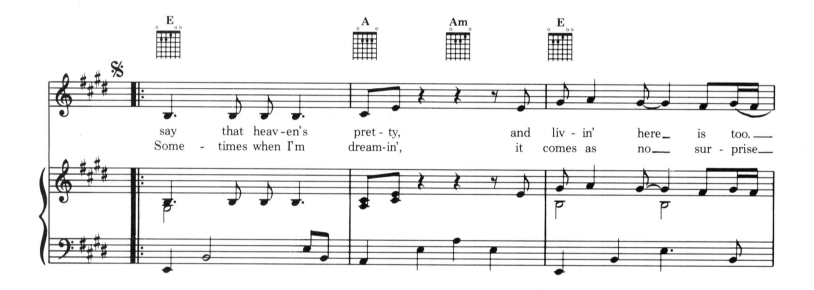

say that heav-en's pret-ty, and liv-in' here is too.
Some - times when I'm dream-in', it comes as no sur-prise

But if they said that I would have to chose
that if you'll look you'll see the home - sick feel-

be - tween ___ the two, ___ I'd ___ go home, ___
- in' in ___ my eyes. ___ I'm go - in' home, ___

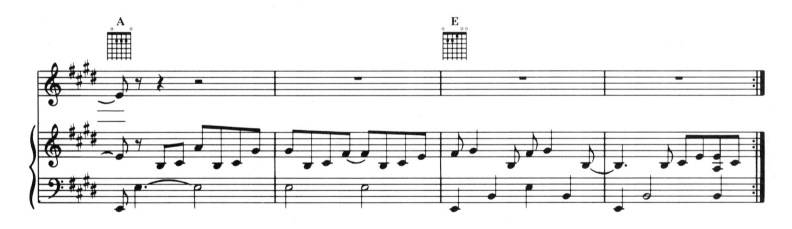

go - in' home, ___ where I be - long. ___
I'm go - in' home, ___ where I be - long. ___

While I'm here ___ I'll serve ___ Him glad - ly, sing Him all ___ these songs ___

I'm here, _____ but not for

long. _____ 4. One day I'll _____ be sleep-

D.S. (3rd verse)
al 2nd ending

-in' when Death knocks on _____ my door, _____ And

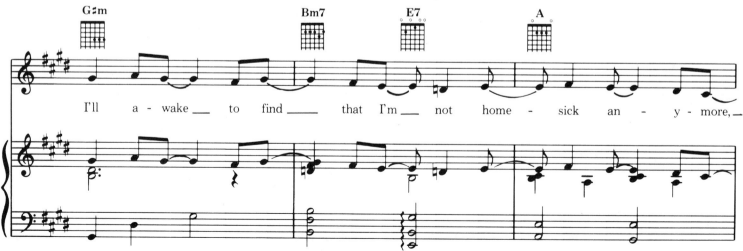

I'll a-wake _____ to find _____ that I'm _____ not home-sick an-y-more, _____

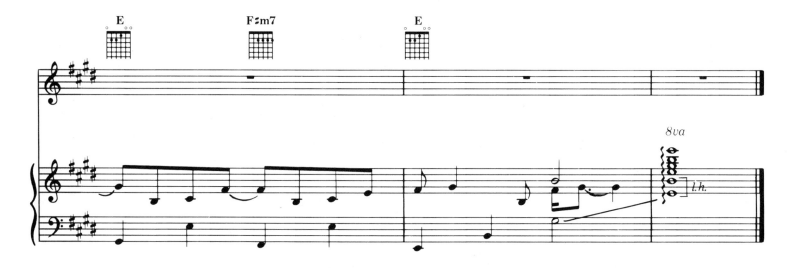

3. When I'm feelin' lonely, and when I'm feelin' blue,
it's such a joy to know that I am only passin' through.
I'm headed home, I'm goin' home, where I belong.

HOW GREAT THOU ART

Words and Music by
STUART K. HINE

*Author's original words are "works" and "mighty."

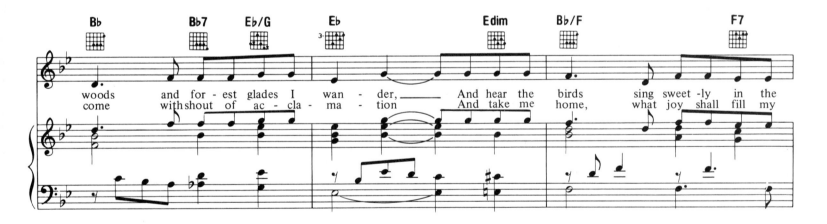

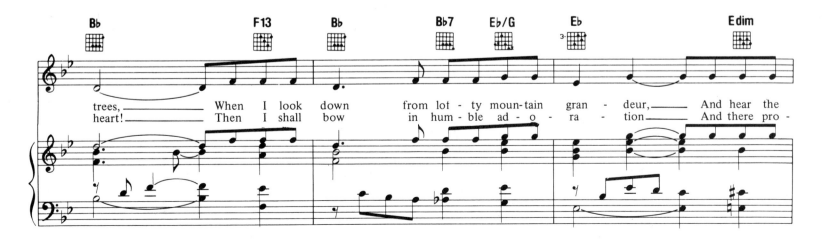

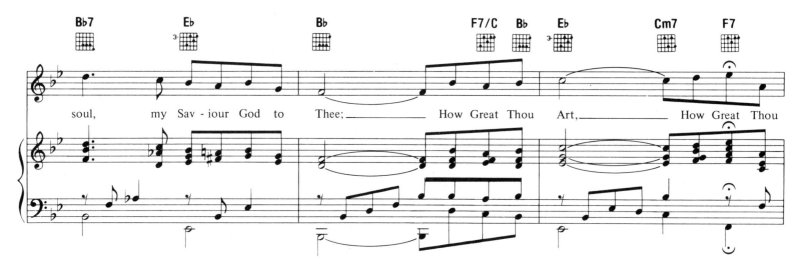

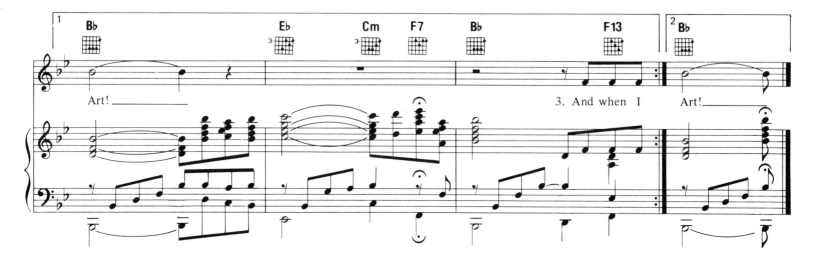

I BOWED ON MY KNEES AND CRIED HOLY

Words by NETTIE DUDLEY WASHINGTON
Music by E.M. DUDLEY CANTWELL

I FEEL LIKE TRAVELING ON

Words and Music by
WILLIAM HUNTER

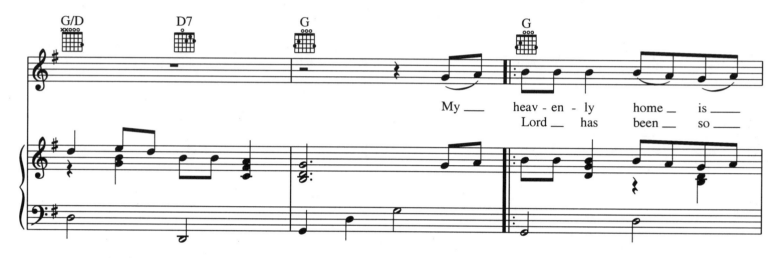

My __ heav - en - ly home __ is __
Lord __ has been __ so __

bright and fair, I __ feel like trav - el - ing
good to me, I feel like trav - el - ing

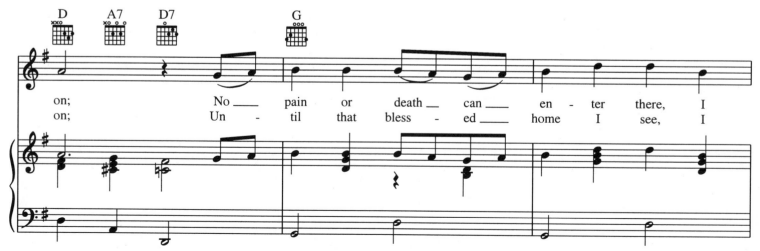

on; No __ pain or death __ can __ en - ter there, I
on; Un - til that bless - ed __ home I see, I

I JUST CAME TO PRAISE THE LORD

Words and Music by WAYNE ROMERO

I JUST FEEL LIKE SOMETHING GOOD IS ABOUT TO HAPPEN

Words and Music by
WILLIAM J. GAITHER

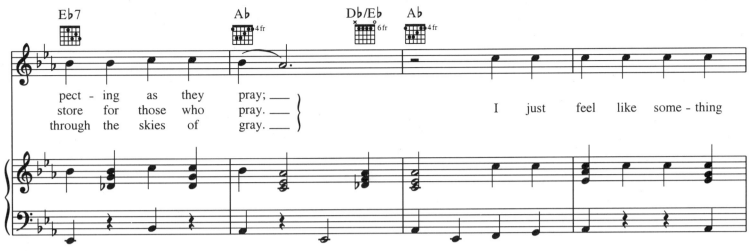

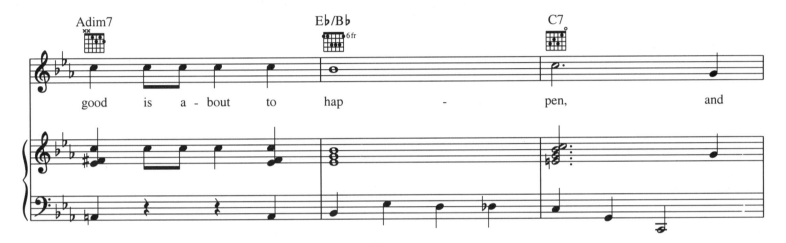

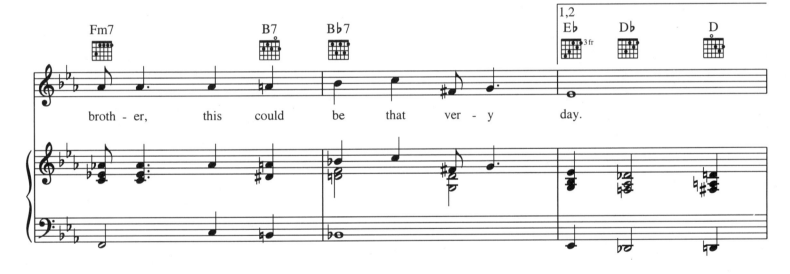

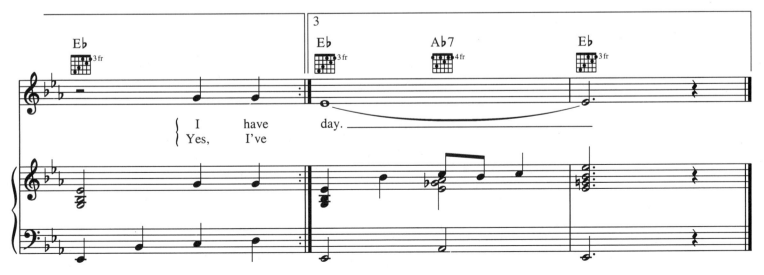

I SAW THE LIGHT

Words and Music by
HANK WILLIAMS

Praise   the   Lord_____   I   Saw   The
Praise   the   Lord_____   I   Saw   The
Praise   the   Lord_____   I   Saw   The

Light.⎫
Light.⎬   I   Saw   The
Light.⎭

Light_____   I   Saw   The   Light._____

No   more   dark - ness,   No   more

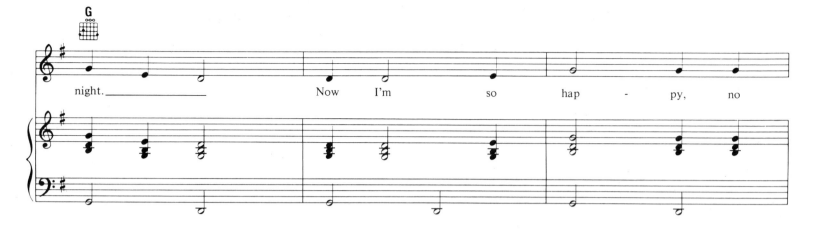

night._____ Now I'm so hap - py, no

sor - row in sight._____ Praise The

Lord_____ I Saw The Light.

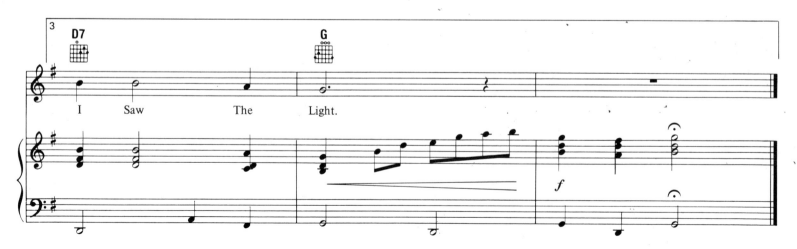

I Saw The Light.

IT'S BEGINNING TO RAIN

Words by GLORIA GAITHER and AARON WILBURN
Music by WILLIAM J. GAITHER and AARON WILBURN

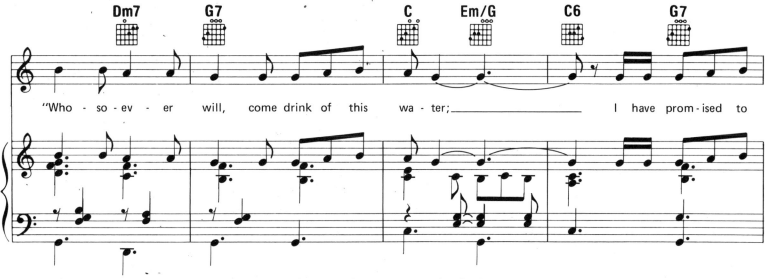

I'D RATHER HAVE JESUS

Words by RHEA F. MILLER
Music by GEORGE BEVERLY SHEA

Warmly

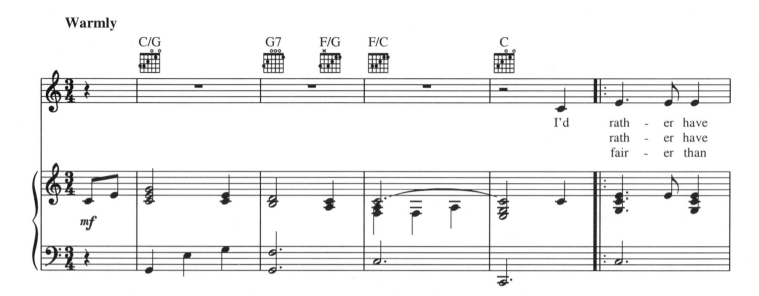

I'd rath - er have
rath - er have
fair - er than

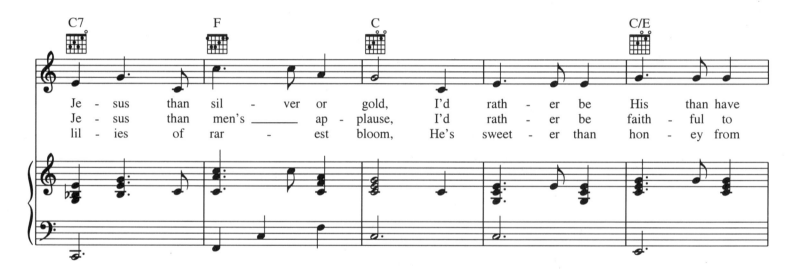

Je - sus than sil - ver or gold, I'd rath - er be His than have
Je - sus than men's _____ ap - plause, I'd rath - er be faith - ful to
lil - ies of rar - est bloom, He's sweet - er than hon - ey from

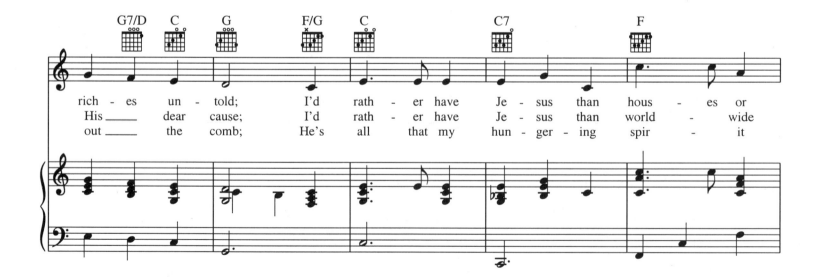

rich - es un - told; I'd rath - er have Je - sus than hous - es or
His _____ dear cause; I'd rath - er have Je - sus than world - wide
out _____ the comb; He's all that my hun - ger - ing spir - it

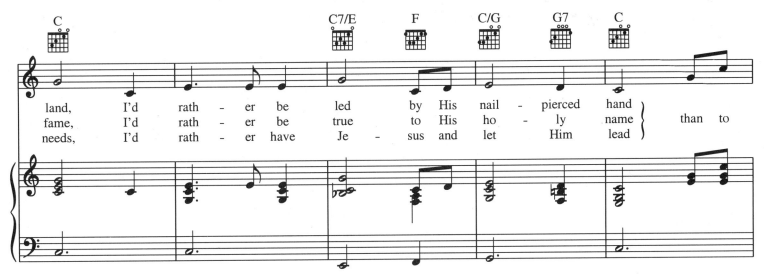

land, I'd rath - er be led by His nail - pierced hand } than to
fame, I'd rath - er be true to His ho - ly name } than to
needs, I'd rath - er have Je - sus and let Him lead }

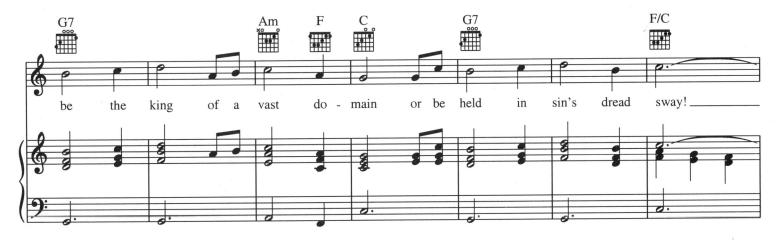

be the king of a vast do - main or be held in sin's dread sway! _____

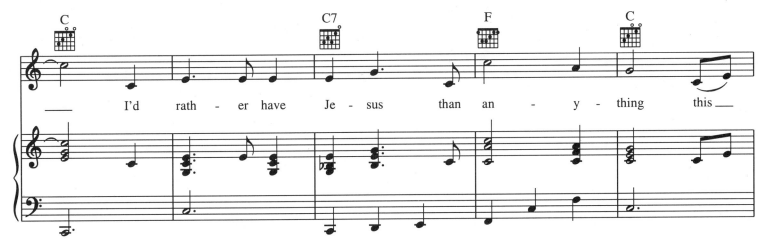

_____ I'd rath - er have Je - sus than an - y - thing this _____

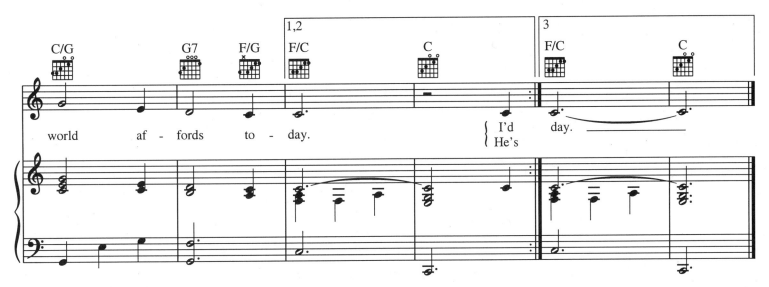

world af - fords to - day.   { I'd day. _____
                                      { He's

I'LL FLY AWAY

Words and Music by
ALBERT E. BRUMLEY

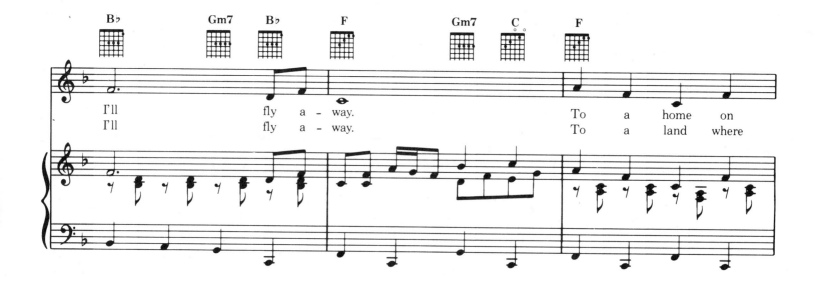

Verse

Some glad morn-ing when this life is o'er, _____
Just a few more wea-ry days and then, _____

I'll fly a-way. To a home on
I'll fly a-way. To a land where

God's ce - les - tial shore, I'll fly a - way.
joy shall nev - er end, I'll fly a - way.

Chorus

I'll fly a - way, O glo - ry, I'll fly a -

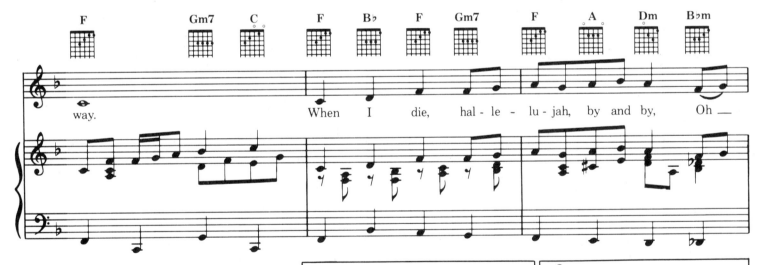

way. When I die, hal - le - lu - jah, by and by, Oh ___

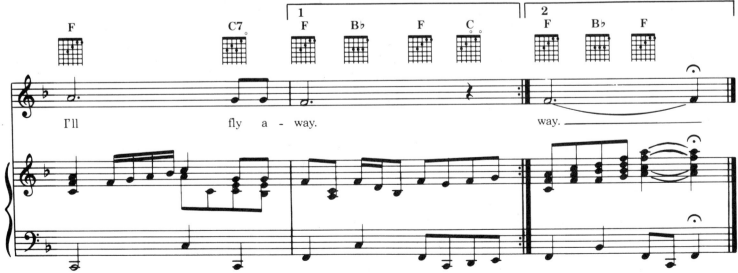

I'll fly a - way. way. ___

IN THE GARDEN

Words and Music by
C. AUSTIN MILES

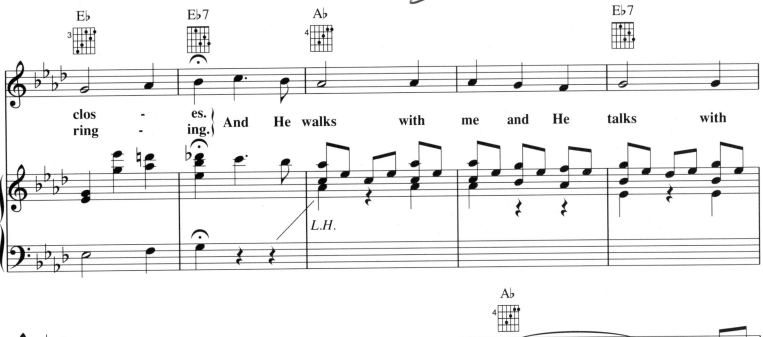

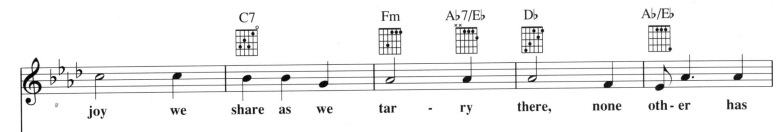

IN TIMES LIKE THESE

Words and Music by
RUTH CAYE JONES

IT IS NO SECRET
(What God Can Do)

Words and Music by
STUART HAMBLEN

MCA Music Publishing

IT TOOK A MIRACLE

Words and Music by
JOHN W. PETERSON

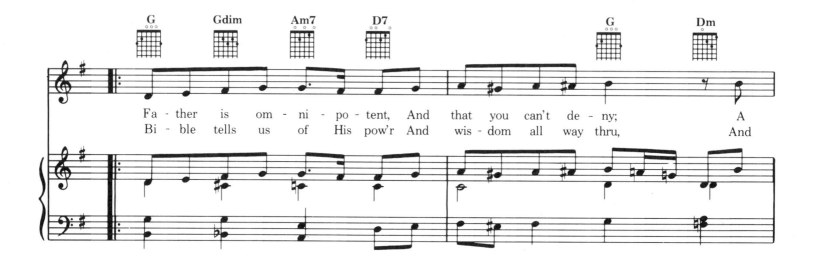

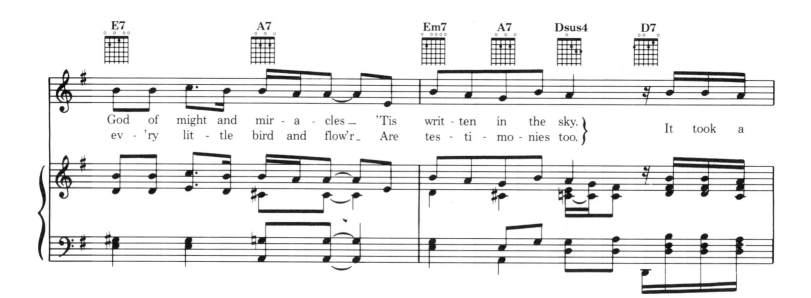

JUST A CLOSER WALK WITH THEE

Traditional
Arranged by KENNETH MORRIS

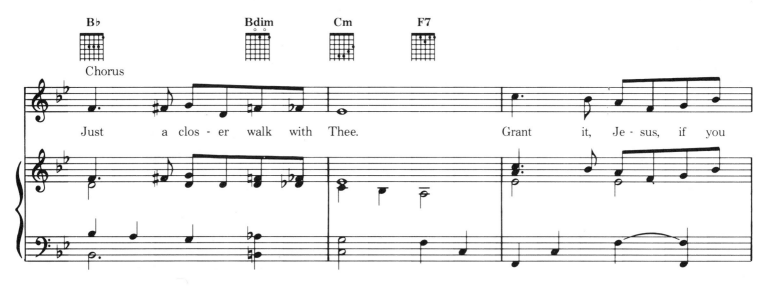

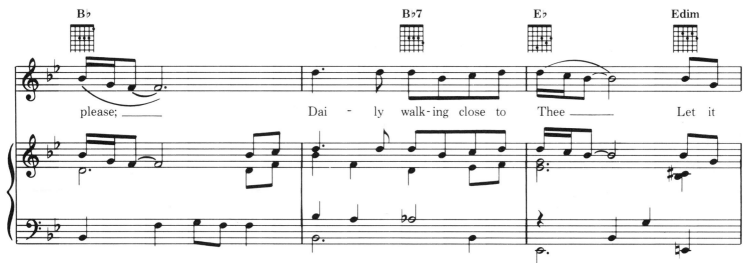

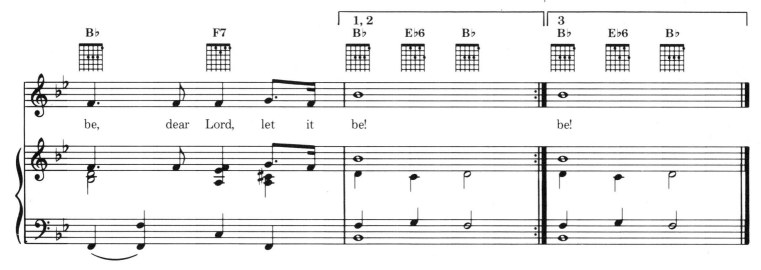

3. When my feeble life is o'er,
Time for me will be no more;
On that bright eternal shore
I will walk, dear Lord, close to Thee.

JUST A LITTLE TALK WITH JESUS

Words and Music by
CLEAVANT DERRICKS

just a lit-tle talk with Je - sus made me whole.
just a lit-tle talk with Je - sus clears the way.
just a lit-tle talk with Je - sus makes it right.

Now let us have a lit-tle talk with Je - sus, let us

tell Him all a-bout our trou-bles, He will hear our faint-est cry and He will an-swer by and by. Now when you

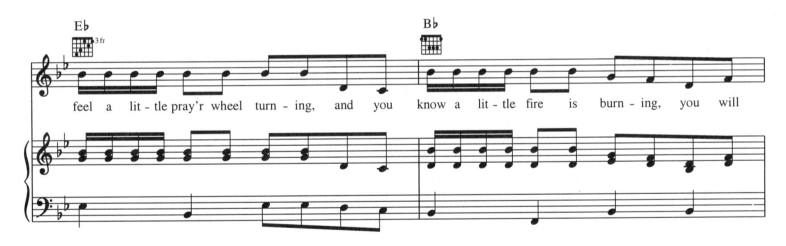

feel a lit-tle pray'r wheel turn - ing, and you know a lit-tle fire is burn-ing, you will

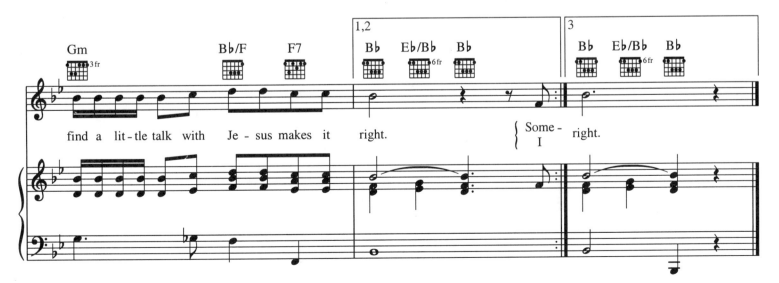

find a lit-tle talk with Je - sus makes it right.

Some - I right.

JUST OVER IN THE GLORYLAND

Words and Music by J.W. ACUFF
and EMMETT DEAN

Additional Lyrics

2. I am on my way to those mansions fair,
    Just over in the glory land;
    There to sing God's praise and His glory share,
    Just over in the glory land.
    REFRAIN

3. What a joyful tho't that my Lord I'll see,
    Just over in the glory land;
    And with kindred saved there forever be,
    Just over in the glory land.
    REFRAIN

4. With the blood-washed throng I will shout and sing,
    Just over in the glory land;
    Glad hosannas to Christ, the Lord and King,
    Just over in the glory land.
    REFRAIN

THE KING IS COMING

Words by WILLIAM J. and GLORIA GAITHER
and CHARLES MILLHUFF
Music by WILLIAM J. GAITHER

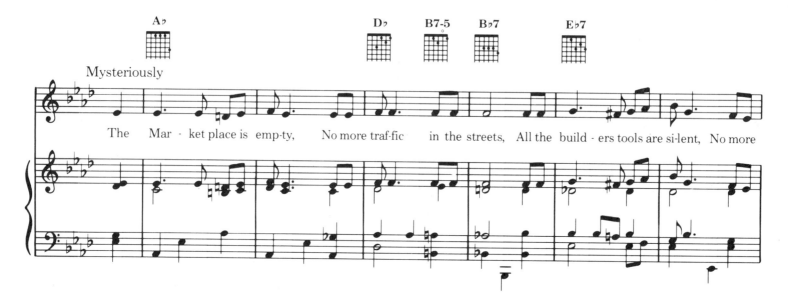

Mysteriously

The Mar-ket place is emp-ty, No more traf-fic in the streets, All the build-ers tools are si-lent, No more

time to har-vest wheat; Bu-sy house-wives cease their la-bors, in the court-room no de-bate, Work on

Intensely

earth is all sus-pend-ed as the King comes thro' the gate. Hap-py fa-ces line the hall-ways. Those whose

MANSION OVER THE HILLTOP

Words and Music by
IRA STANPHILL

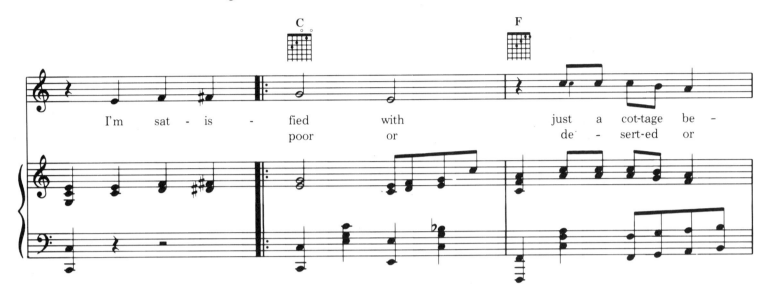

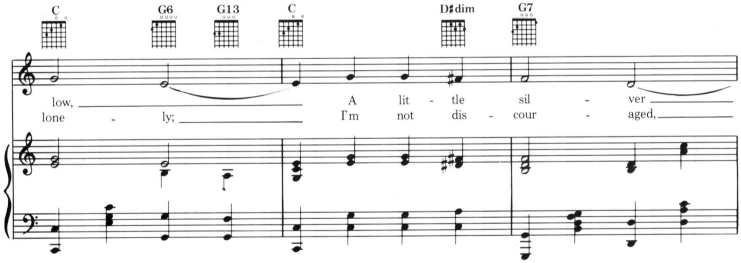

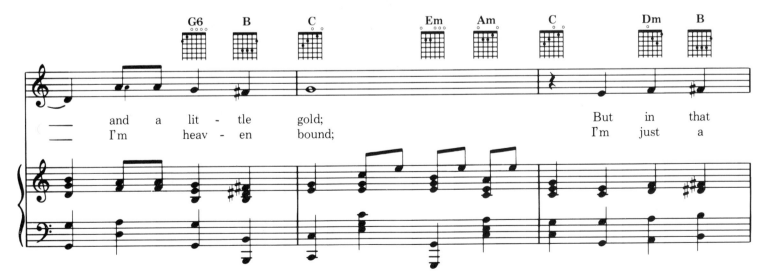

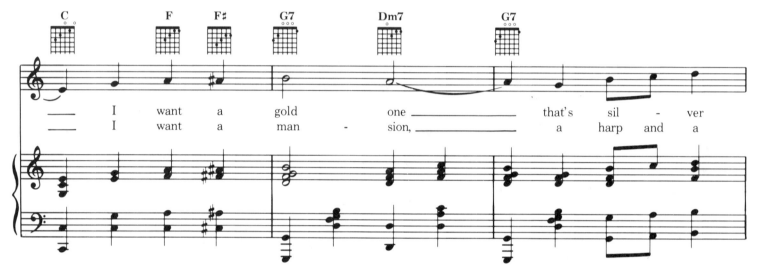

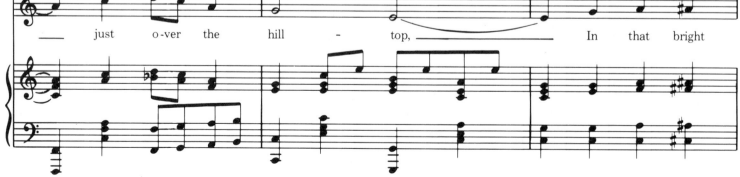

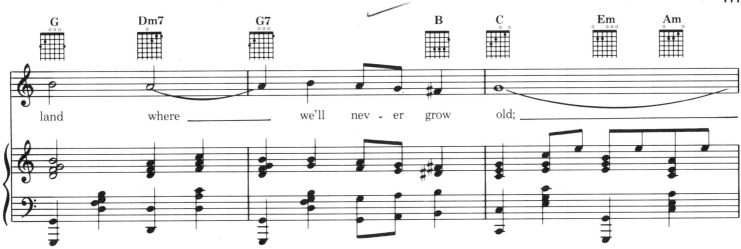

land where _____ we'll nev-er grow old; _____

_____ And some-day yon - der _____ we will nev-er-more

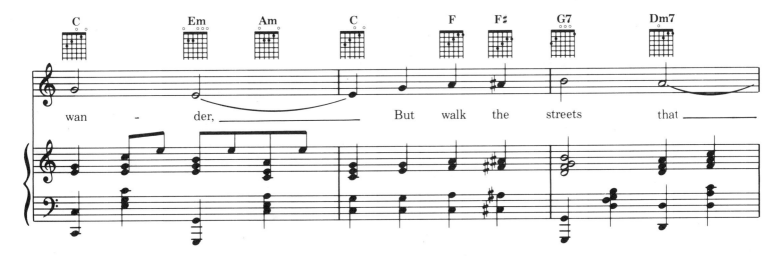

wan - der, _____ But walk the streets that _____

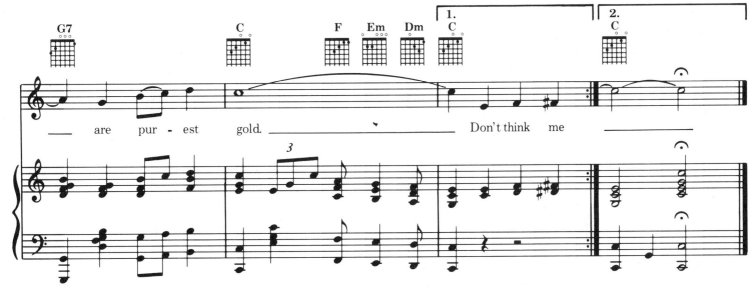

_____ are pur-est gold. _____ Don't think me

LIFT HIM UP

Words and Music by
DON JARVIS

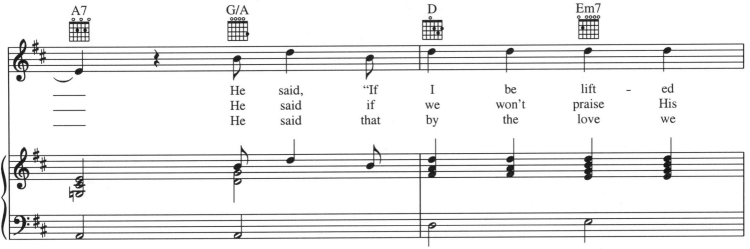

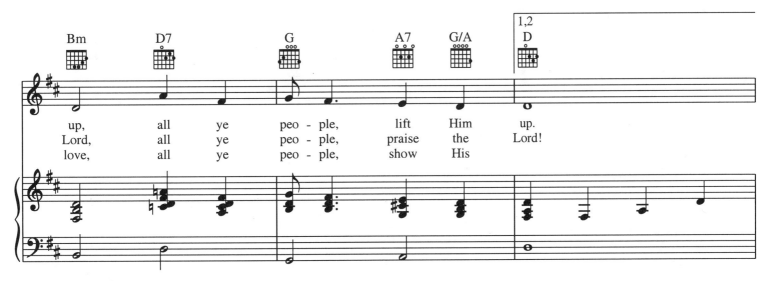

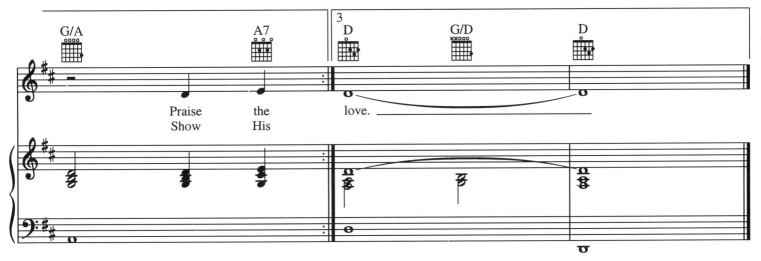

THE LILY OF THE VALLEY

Words by CHARLES W. FRY
Music by WILLIAM S. HAYS

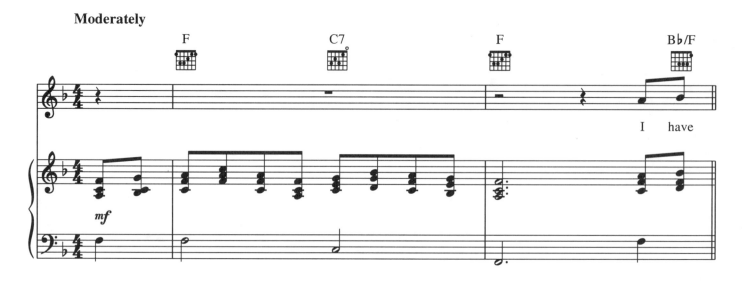

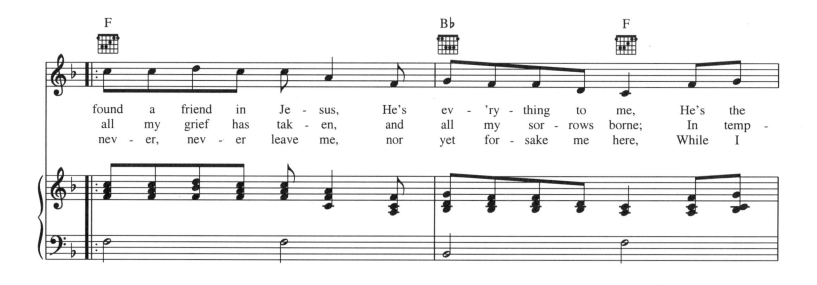

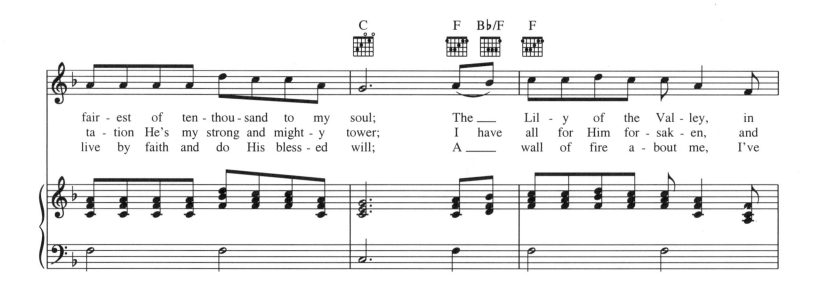

115

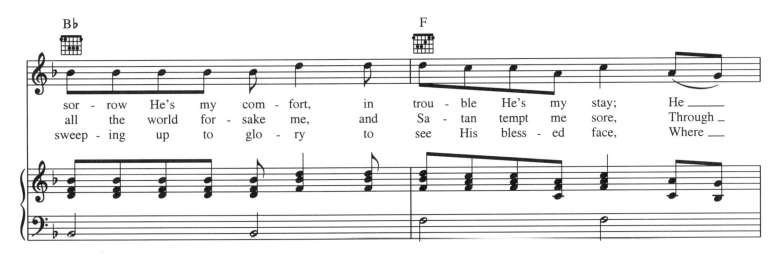

THE LONGER I SERVE HIM

Words and Music by
WILLIAM J. GAITHER

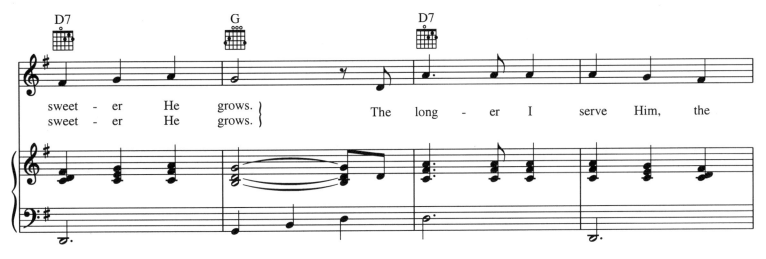

sweet - er He grows.
sweet - er He grows. } The long - er I serve Him, the

sweet - er He grows, The more that I love Him, more love He be -

stows. Each day is like heav - en, my heart o - ver - flows, The

long - er I serve __ Him, the sweet - er He grows. grows.

MIDNIGHT CRY

Words and Music by GREG DAY
and CHUCK DAY

to meet Him in the air. _____ But then those that re-

main _____ will be quick-ly changed _____

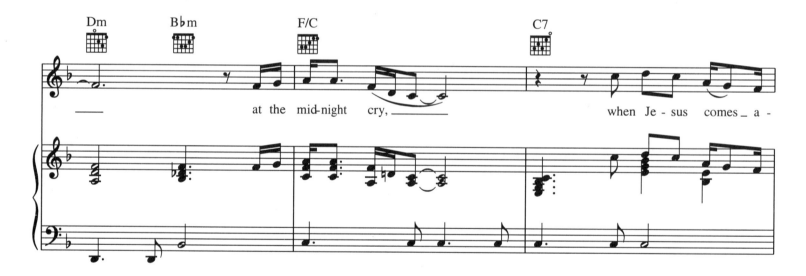

_____ at the mid-night cry, _____ when Je-sus comes_ a-

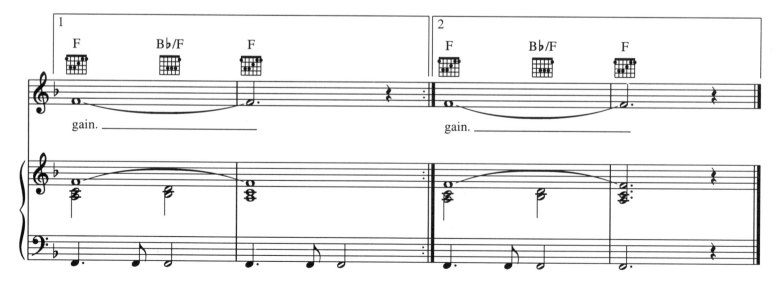

gain. _____   gain. _____

MOVIN' UP TO GLORYLAND

Words and Music by
LEE ROY ABERNATHY

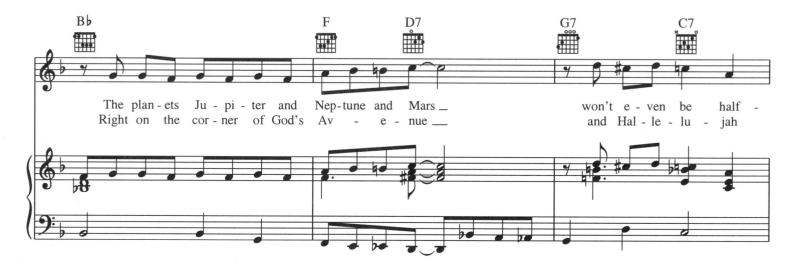

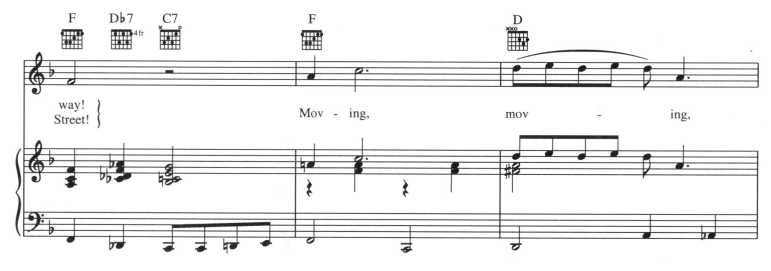

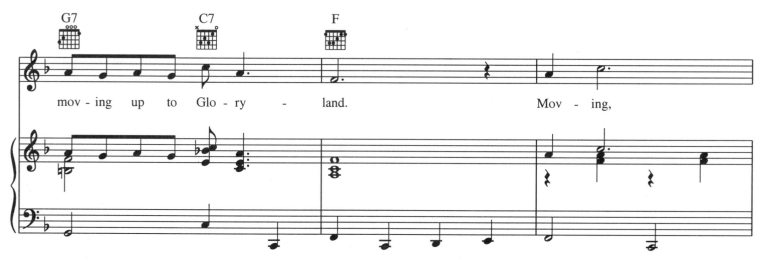

MORE THAN WONDERFUL

Words and Music by
LANNY WOLFE

With expression

He prom-ised us ___ that He would be a Coun - sel-or, a

Might - y God ___ and a Prince of Peace. He prom-ised us ___ that He would be a

Fa - ther and would love us with a love that would not cease. Well, I

heart can be-lieve, He goes be - yond _____ my high - est hopes and fond - est

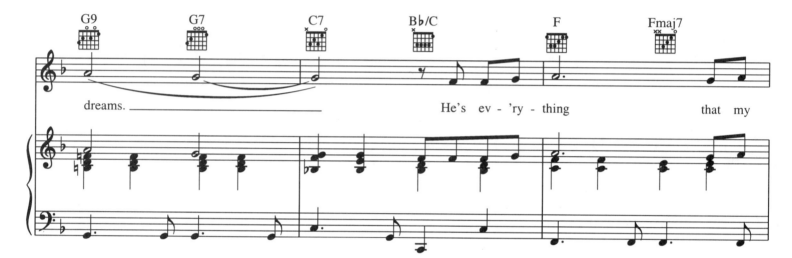

dreams. _____ He's ev - 'ry - thing that my

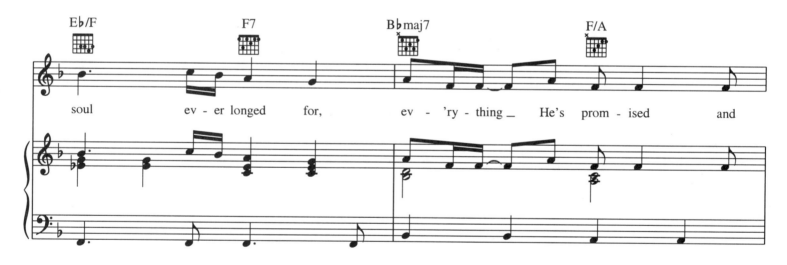

soul ev - er longed for, ev - 'ry - thing_ He's prom - ised and

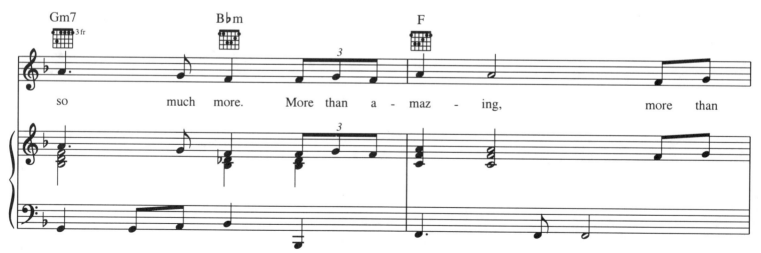

so much more. More than a - maz - ing, more than

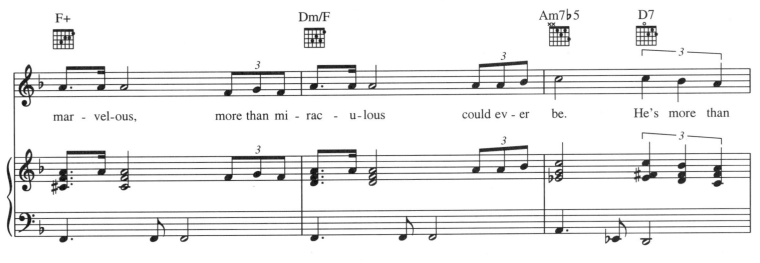

mar - vel-ous, more than mi - rac - u-lous could ev - er be. He's more than

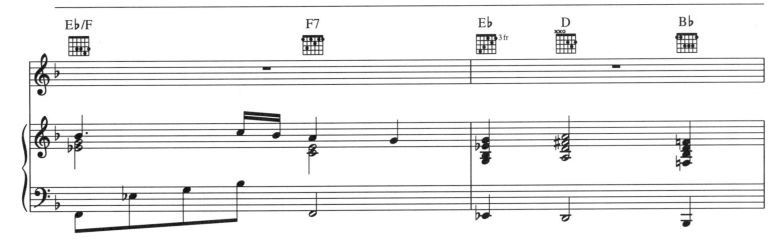

won - der-ful; that's what Je - sus is to me.

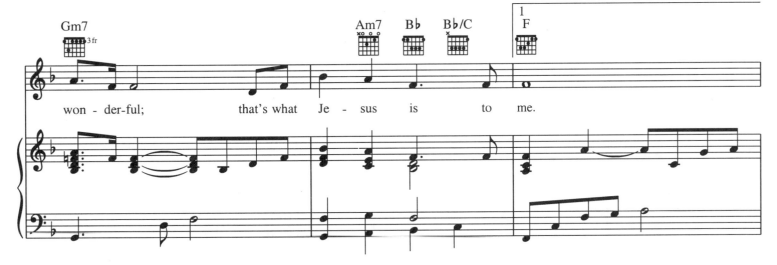

I me.

MY SAVIOR FIRST OF ALL

Words by FANNY J. CROSBY
Music by JOHN R. SWENEY

129

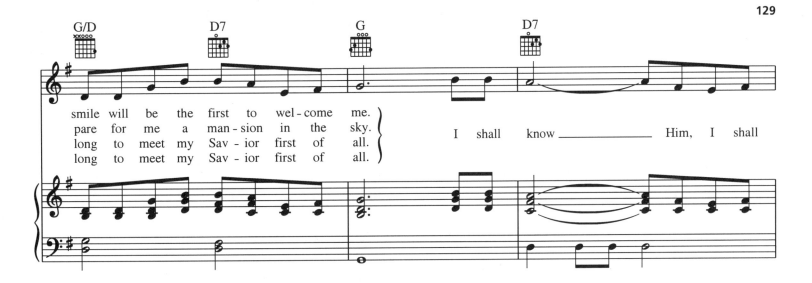

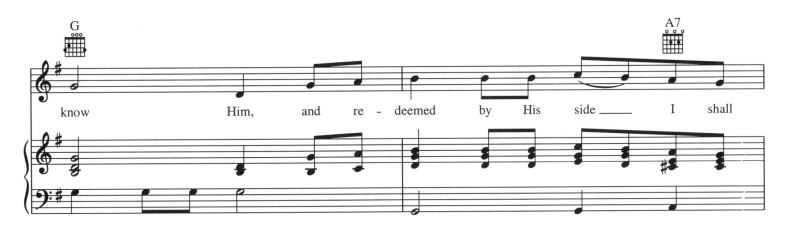

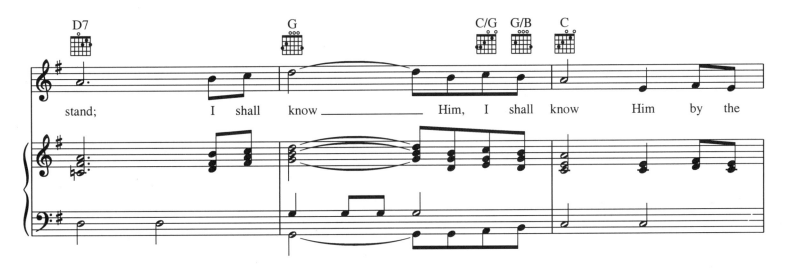

MY TRIBUTE

Words and Music by
ANDRAÉ CROUCH

How _____ can I say thanks for the things You have done for me? Things__ so un-de-served

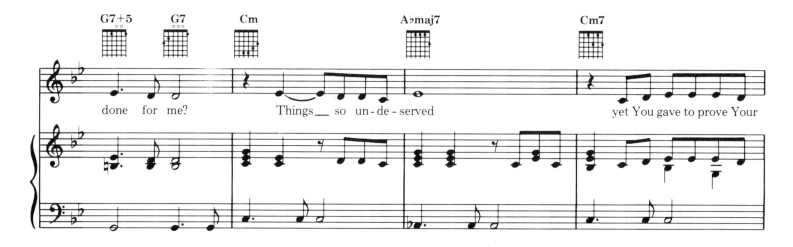

yet You gave to prove Your love for me. The voic-es of a mil-lion an – gels__

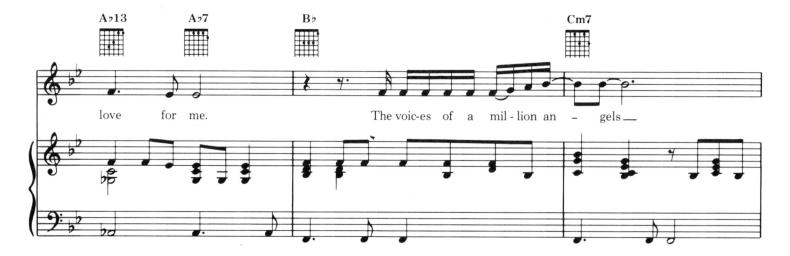

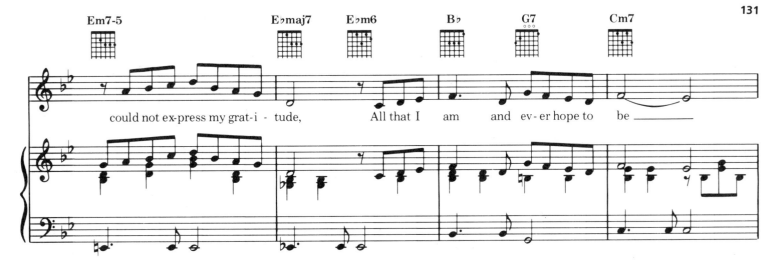

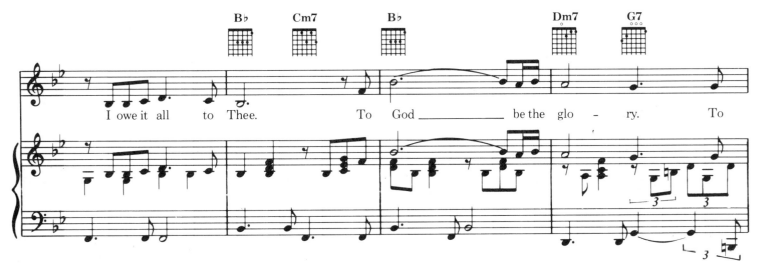

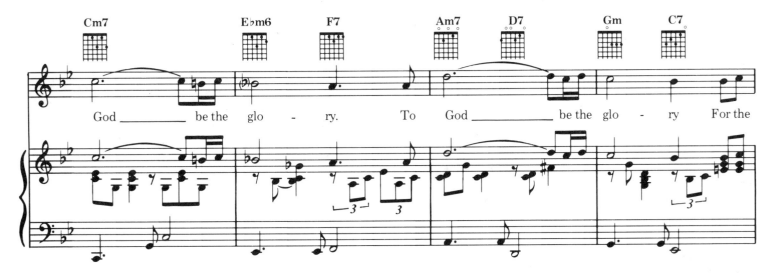

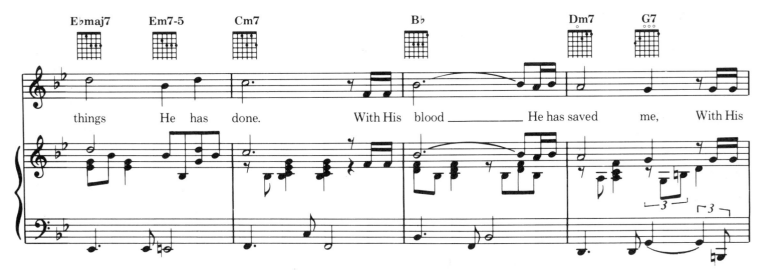

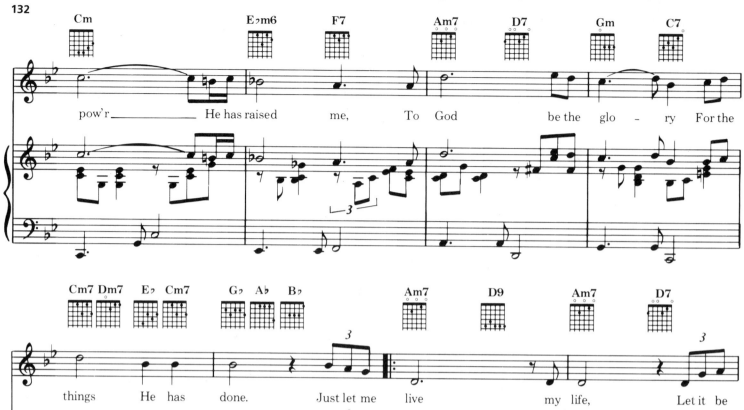

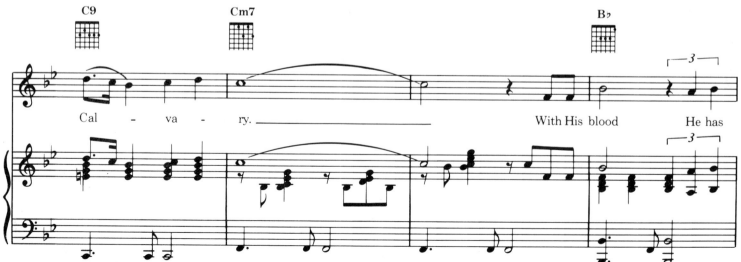

NOW I BELONG TO JESUS

Words and Music by
NORMAN J. CLAYTON

Moderately

Je - sus my Lord will
Once I was lost in
Joy floods my soul for

love me for - ev - er, From Him no pow'r of e - vil can sev - er.
sin's deg - ra - da - tion; Je - sus came down to bring me sal - va - tion,
Je - sus has saved me, Freed me from sin that long had en - slaved me.

He gave His life to ran - som my soul;
Lift - ed me up from sor - row and shame; } Now I be - long to
His pre - cious blood He gave to re - deem; }

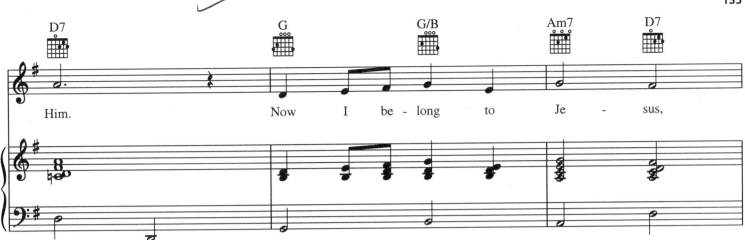

Him. Now I be - long to Je - sus,

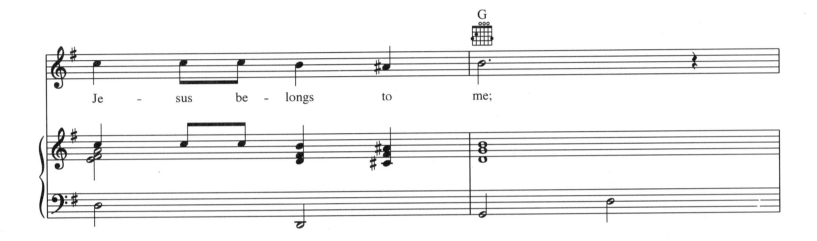

Je - sus be - longs to me;

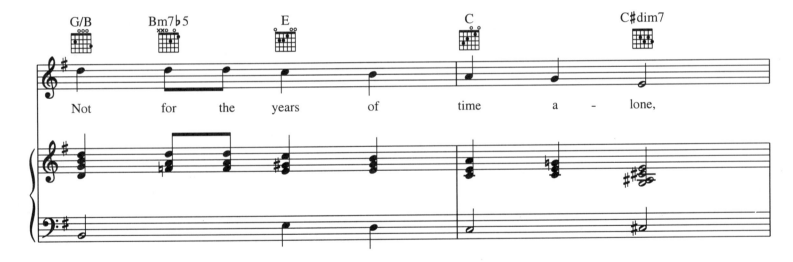

Not for the years of time a - lone,

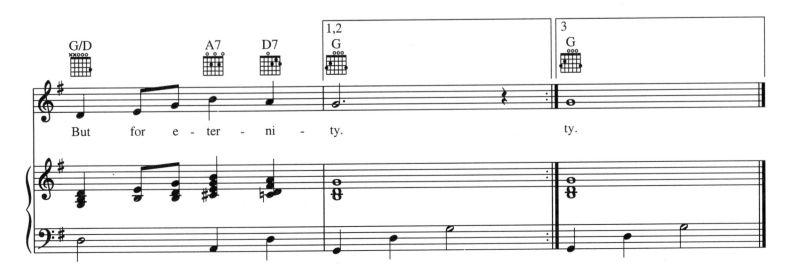

But for e - ter - ni - ty. ty.

THE OLD RUGGED CROSS

By REV. GEORGE BENNARD

PART THE WATERS

Words and Music by
CHARLES F. BROWN

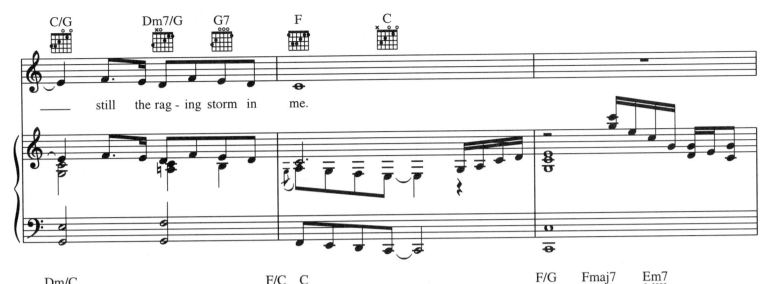

still the rag - ing storm in me.

{ Know-ing you

{ Know-ing you

love me _____ through the bur - dens I must _ bear, hear - ing your

love me _____ helps me face an - oth - er _____ day, hear - ing your

foot - steps _____ lets me know I'm in _____ your care, and in the

foot - steps _____ drives the clouds and fears _ a - way, and in the

sea. When I cry for help, __ O hear me, Lord, __ and

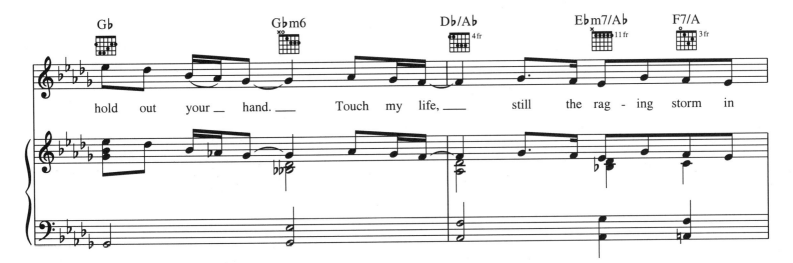

hold out your __ hand. __ Touch my life, __ still the rag - ing storm in

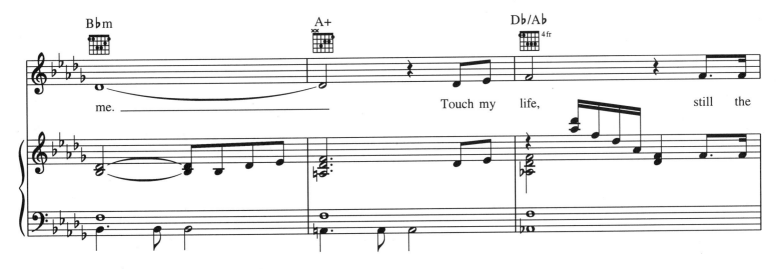

me. __ Touch my life, still the

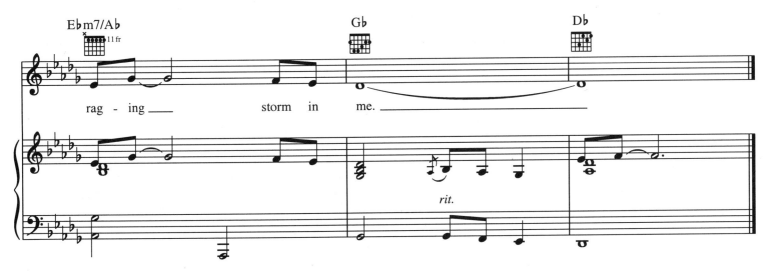

rag - ing __ storm in me. __

(There'll Be)
PEACE IN THE VALLEY
(For Me)

Words and Music by
THOMAS A. DORSEY

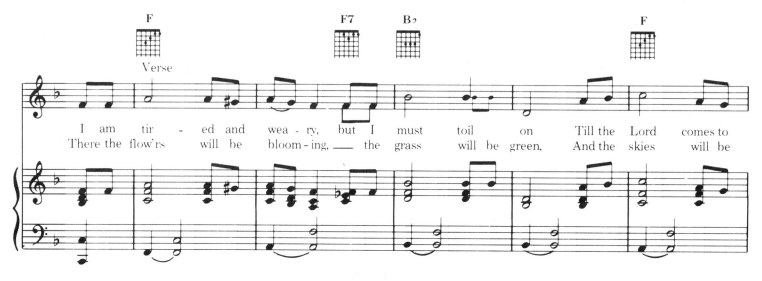

I am tir - ed and wea - ry, but I must toil on Till the Lord comes to
There the flow'rs will be bloom - ing, __ the grass will be green, And the skies will be

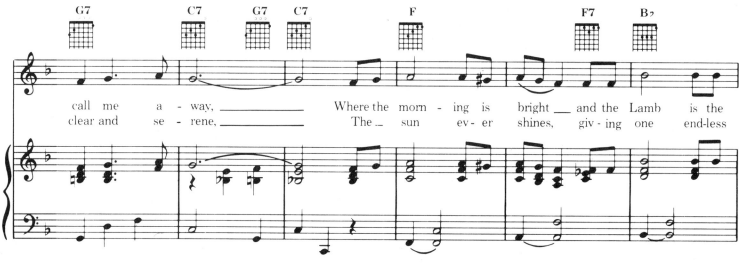

call me a - way, _____ Where the morn - ing is bright __ and the Lamb is the
clear and se - rene, _____ The __ sun ev - er shines, giv - ing one end - less

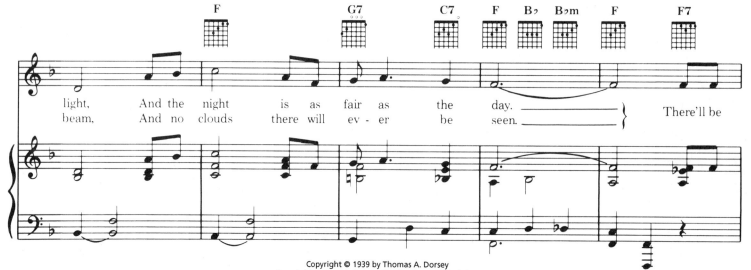

light, And the night is as fair as the day. _____ } There'll be
beam, And no clouds is there will ev - er be seen. _____

3. There the bear will be gentle, the wolf will be tame,
And the lion will lay down by the lamb,
The host from the wild will be led by a Child,
I'll be changed from the creature I am.

4. No headaches or heartaches or misunderstands,
No confusion or trouble won't be,
No frowns to defile, just a long endless smile,
There'll be peace and contentment for me.

PRECIOUS LORD, TAKE MY HAND
(Take My Hand, Precious Lord)

Words and Music by
THOMAS A. DORSEY

Pre-cious Lord take my hand lead me on, let me stand,— I am tired,— I am weak, I am worn.— Thru the storm, thru the night lead me on to the light,— Take My Hand,— Pre-cious Lord— lead me home.—

145

PRECIOUS MEMORIES

Words and Music by
J.B.F. WRIGHT

Pre - cious mem-'ries, un - seen
Pre - cious fa - ther. lov - ing

an - gels, Sent From _ some-where to my
moth - er, Fly a - cross the lone - ly

soul; _____
years; _____

3. As I travel on life's pathway, I know not what life shall hold;
   As I wander hopes grow fonder, Precious mem'ries flood my soul.

RISE AGAIN

Words and Music by
DALLAS HOLM

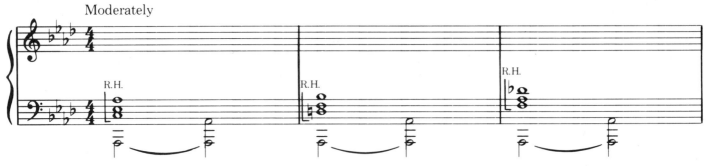

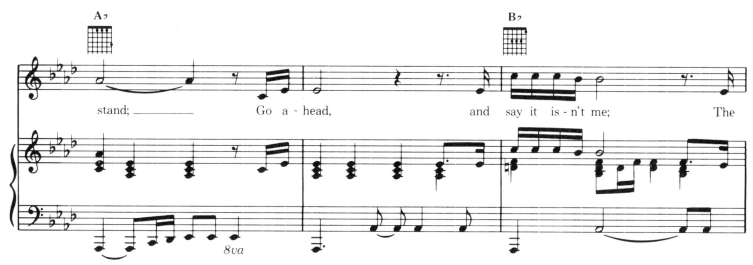

stand; _____ Go a-head, and say it is-n't me; The

day __ will come __ when you __ will see! _____ 'Cause I'll

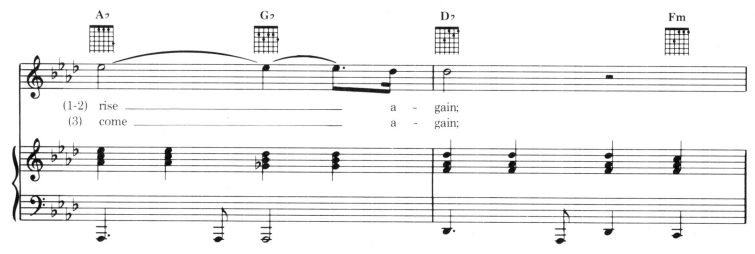

(1-2) rise _____ a - gain;
(3) come _____ a - gain;

Ain't no pow'r on __ earth can tie __ me down; __ Yes, I'll
Ain't no pow'r on __ earth can keep __ me back; __ Yes, I'll

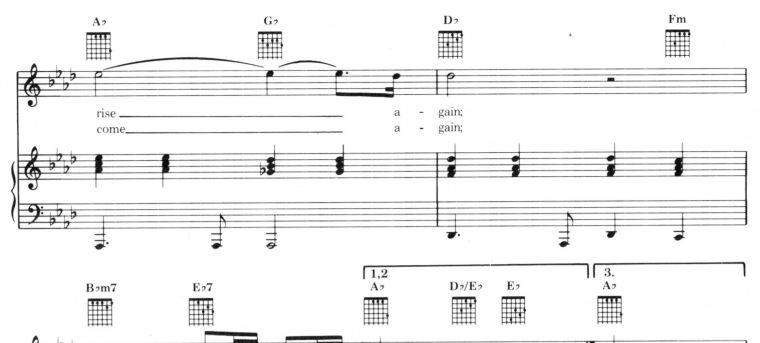

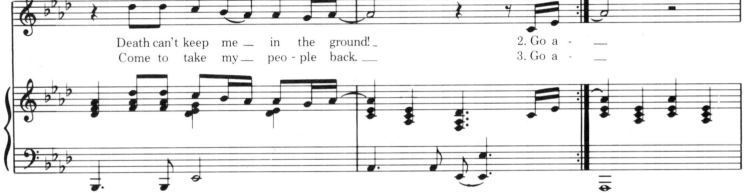

2. Go ahead, and mock my name; My love for you is still the same;
   Go ahead and bury me; But very soon I will be free!
   'Cause I'll . . . (*chorus*)

3. Go ahead and say I'm dead and gone, But you will see that you were wrong
   Go ahead, try to hide the Son, But all will see that I'm the One!
   'Cause I'll . . . (*chorus*)

SEND THE LIGHT

Words and Music by
CHARLES GABRIEL

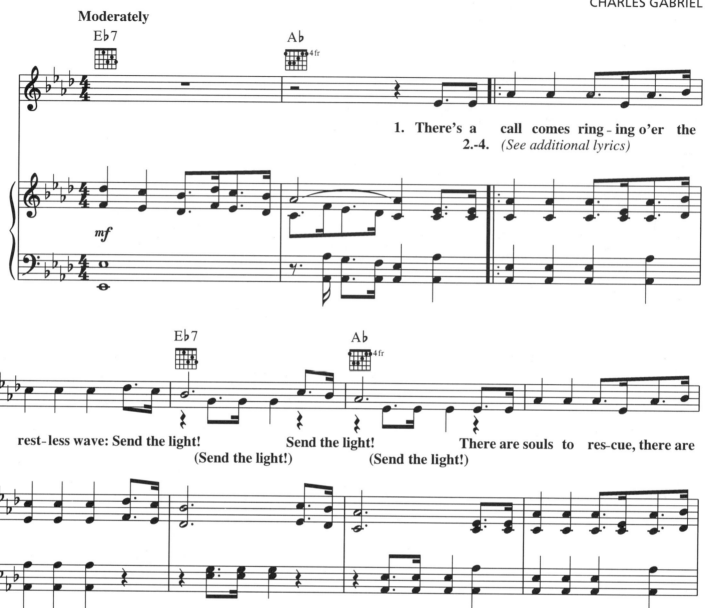

1. There's a call comes ring-ing o'er the
2.-4. *(See additional lyrics)*

rest-less wave: Send the light! Send the light! There are souls to res-cue, there are
(Send the light!) (Send the light!)

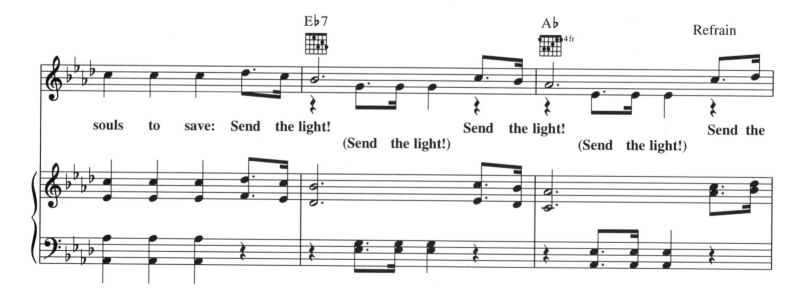

souls to save: Send the light! Send the light! Send the
(Send the light!) (Send the light!)

Additional Lyrics

2. We have heard the Macedonian call today:
Send the light! Send the light!
And a golden off'ring at the cross we lay:
Send the light! Send the light!
REFRAIN

3. Let us pray that grace may ev'rywhere abound:
Send the light! Send the light!
And a Christ-like spirit ev'rywhere be found:
Send the light! Send the light!
REFRAIN

4. Let us not grow weary in the work of love:
Send the light! Send the light!
Let us gather jewels for a crown above:
Send the light! Send the light!
REFRAIN

SHELTERED IN THE ARMS OF GOD

Words and Music by DOTTIE RAMBO
and JIMMIE DAVIS

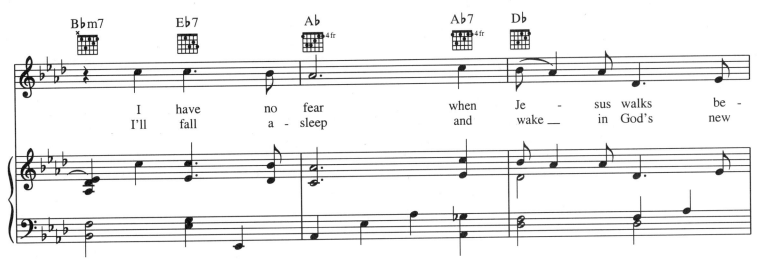
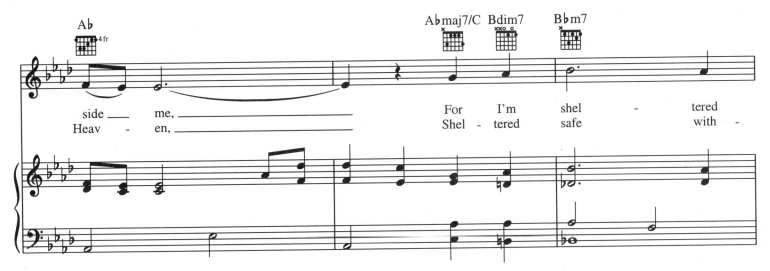
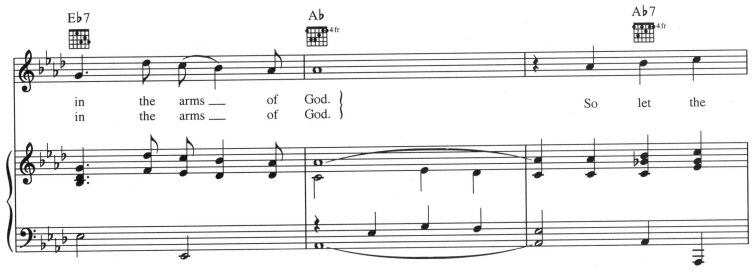
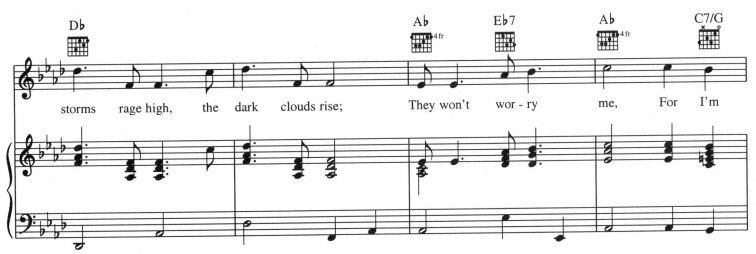

shel - tered safe with - in the arms ___ of God.

He walks with me, and naught _ of earth shall harm _ me, ___

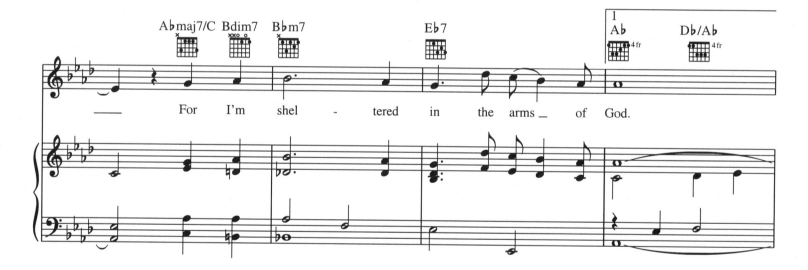

___ For I'm shel - tered in the arms _ of God.

Soon I shall God. ___

SOMETHING BEAUTIFUL

Words by GLORIA GAITHER
Music by WILLIAM J. GAITHER

158

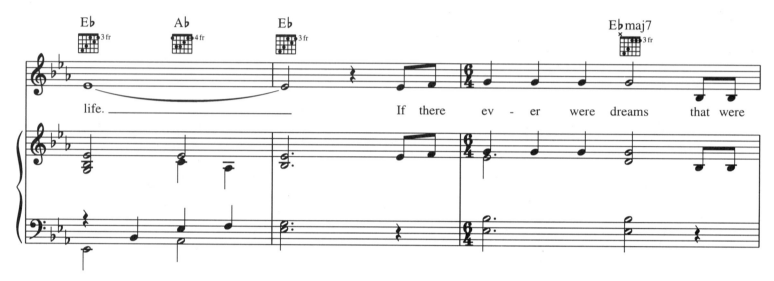

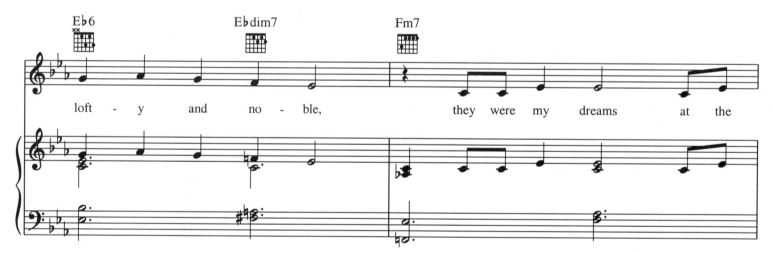

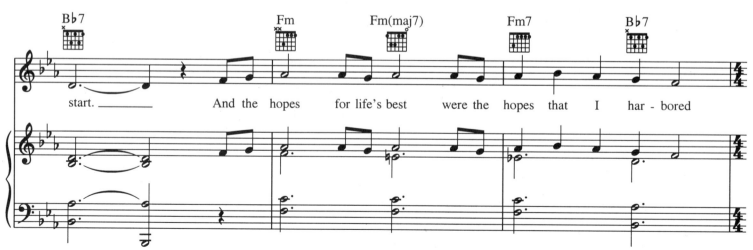

SOON AND VERY SOON

Words and Music by
ANDRAÉ CROUCH

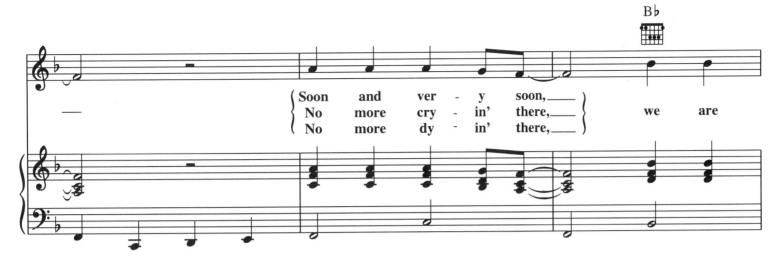

Soon and ver - y soon,____
No more cry - in' there,____
No more dy - in' there,____
we are

goin' to see the king. ____ Hal - le - lu - jah, ____ hal - le -

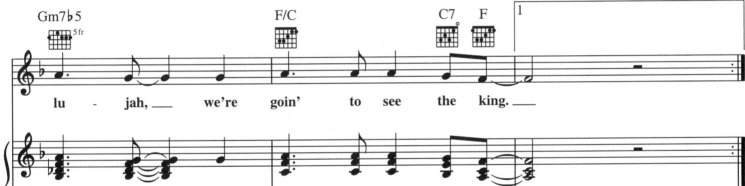

lu - jah, ____ we're goin' to see the king. ____

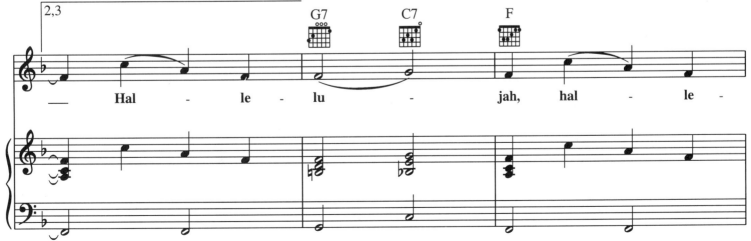

____ Hal - le - lu - jah, hal - le -

lu - jah, hal - le - lu -

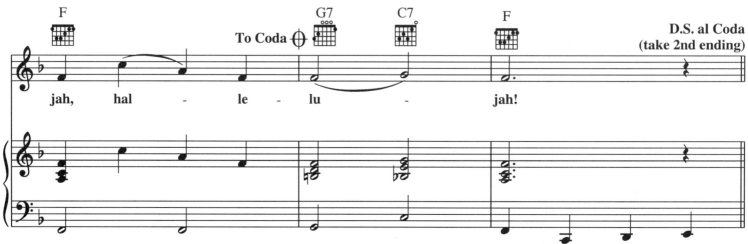

jah, hal - le - lu - jah!

D.S. al Coda
(take 2nd ending)

To Coda

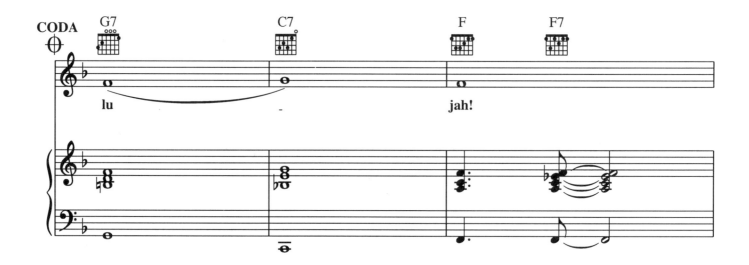

CODA

lu - jah!

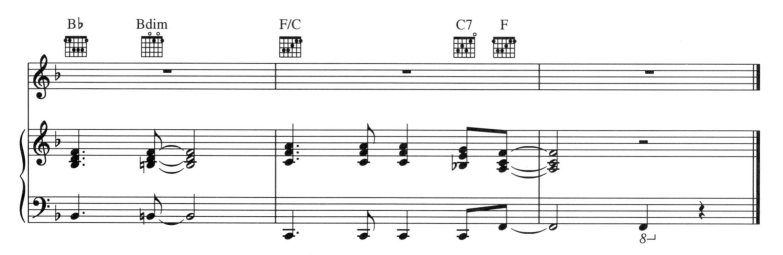

STEPPING ON THE CLOUDS

Words and Music by
LINDA STALLS

Moderately, in 2

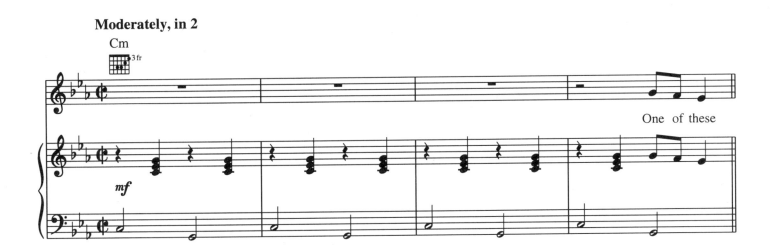

One of these

days _____ I'm gon-na leave, _____ one of these
moon, the stars and the plan-ets, _____ I'm gon-na

days _____ I'm go-ing home; _____
walk on the milk-y white way; _____

I'm gon - na take _____ my fi - nal
When old ___ Ga - briel _____ gives the

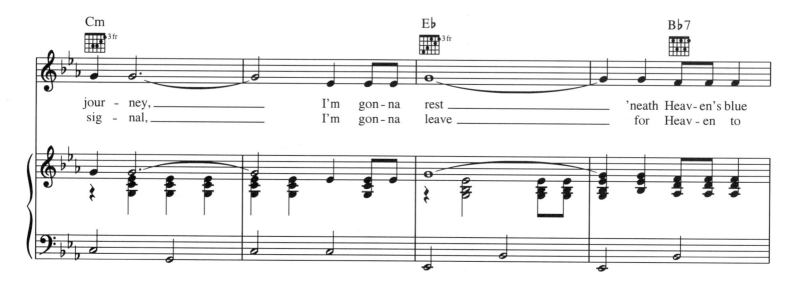

jour - ney, _____ I'm gon - na rest _____ 'neath Heav - en's blue
sig - nal, _____ I'm gon - na leave _____ for Heav - en to

dome. _____
stay. _____ Step - ping on the clouds, we'll see Je - sus,

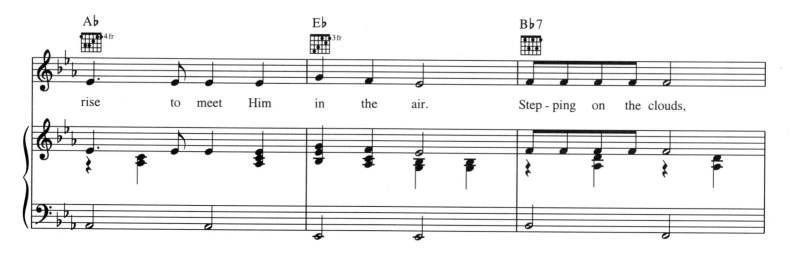

rise to meet Him in the air. Step - ping on the clouds,

He will greet us, oh, the joy to-geth-er we'll share! _____

_____ I'm gon-na leave this world be-hind me, go-ing where the dev-il can-not

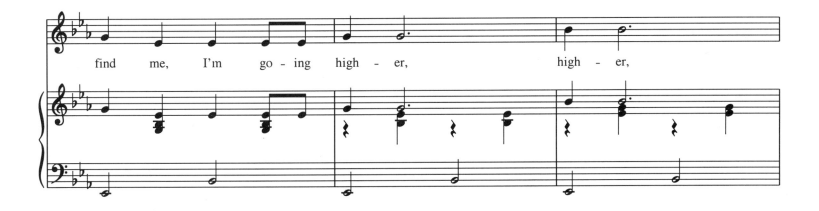

find me, I'm go-ing high-er, high - er,

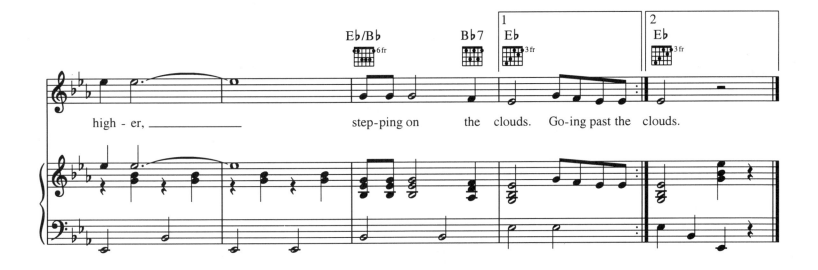

high - er, _____ step-ping on the clouds. Go-ing past the clouds.

SURELY THE PRESENCE OF THE LORD IS IN THIS PLACE

Words and Music by
LANNY WOLFE

Gracefully

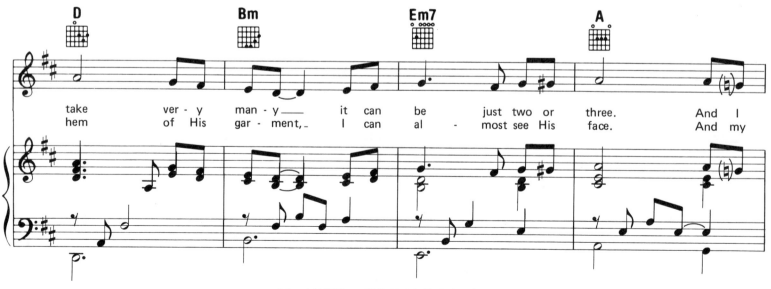

THERE'S SOMETHING ABOUT THAT NAME

Words by WILLIAM J. and GLORIA GAITHER
Music by WILLIAM J. GAITHER

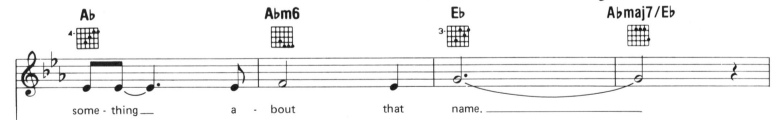

Je - sus, Je - sus, Je - sus; There's just
(recitation 1)
(recitation 2)

some - thing a - bout that name.

RECITATION

1. Jesus, the mere mention of His Name can calm the storm,
heal the broken, raise the dead. At the Name of Jesus, I've seen sin-
hardened men melted, derelicts transformed, the lights of hope put
back into the eyes of a hopeless child. . .

At the Name of Jesus, hatred and bitterness turned to love and
forgiveness, arguments cease.

I've heard a mother softly breathe His Name at the bedside of
a child delirious from fever, and I've watched that little body grow
quiet and the fevered brow cool.

I've sat beside a dying saint, her body racked with pain, who
in those final fleeting seconds summoned her last ounce of ebbing
strength to whisper earth's sweetest Name - Jesus, Jesus. . .

2. Emperors have tried to destroy it; philosophies have tried to
stamp it out. Tyrants have tried to wash it from the face of the earth
with the very blood of those who claimed it. Yet still it stands.

And there shall be that final day when every voice that has
ever uttered a sound - every voice of Adam's race shall raise in one
great mighty chorus to proclaim the Name of Jesus - for in that day
"Every knee shall bow and every tongue shall confess that Jesus Chirst
is Lord!!!"

Ah - so you see - it was not mere chance that caused the
angel one night long ago to say to a virgin maiden, "His Name shall
be called Jesus." Jesus - Jesus - Jesus. You know, there is something
about that Name. . .

'TIL THE STORM PASSES BY

Words and Music by
MOSIE LISTER

clouds roll for - ev - er from the sky, _____ Hold me

fast, let me stand in the hol - low of Thy

hand; Keep me safe 'til the storm pass - es

by. _____ { Man - y / When the } by. _____

TURN YOUR RADIO ON

Words and Music by
ALBERT BRUMLEY

bra - tions com - ing from the joy that His love can bring, Turn your ra - di - o on, _____
liev - er lean - in' on the truths that were nev - er false, Get in touch with God, _____

Turn your ra - di - o on. _____
Turn your ra - di - o on. _____ Turn your ra - di - o

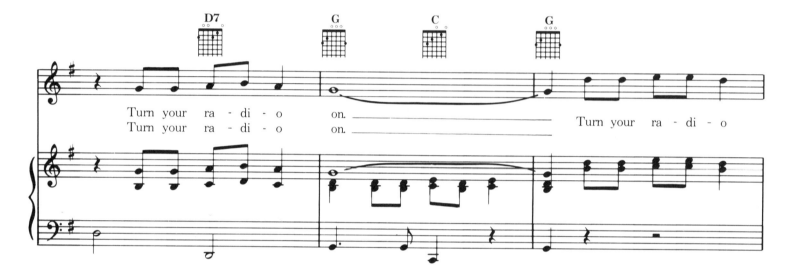

on _____ and lis - ten to the mu - sic in the air, _____ Turn your ra - di - o

on, _____ heav - en's glo - ry share. _____

Turn your lights down low ___ and lis-ten to the Mas-ter's ra - di - o ___

Get in touch with God _____ Turn your ra - di - o

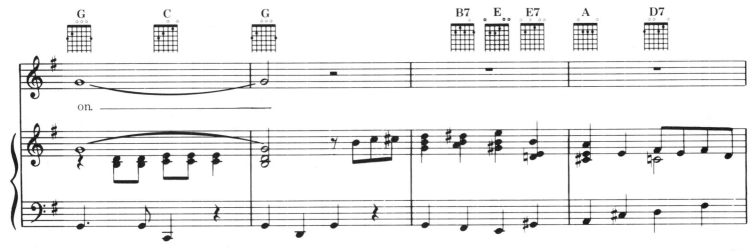

on. _____

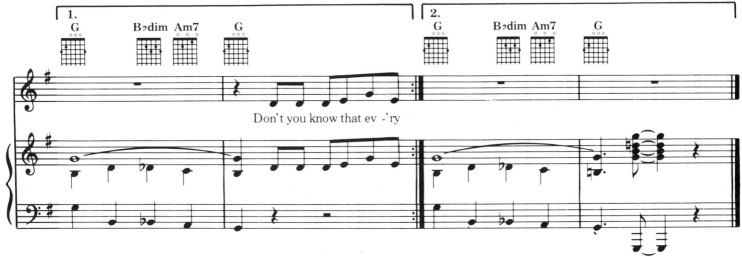

Don't you know that ev -'ry

UNCLOUDED DAY

Words and Music by
J.K. ALWOOD

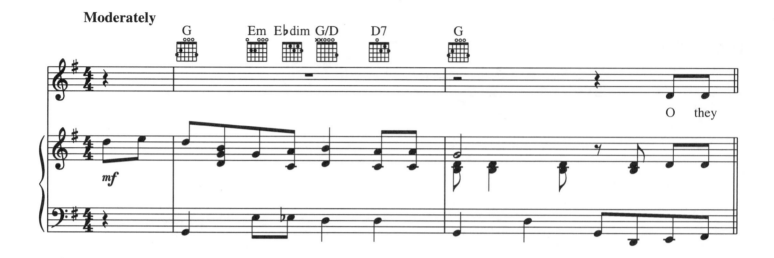

UPON THIS ROCK

Words by GLORIA GAITHER
Music by DONY McGUIRE

186

stand the storms of time.___ Up-on this Rock,_____

___ I'll build My___ church. Up-on this Rock,_____

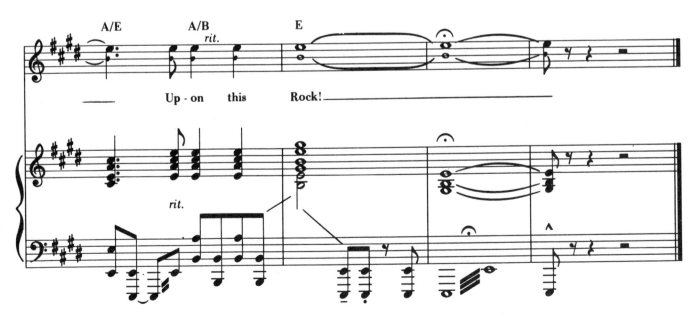

___ Up - on this Rock!_____

VICTORY IN JESUS

Words and Music by
E.M. BARTLETT

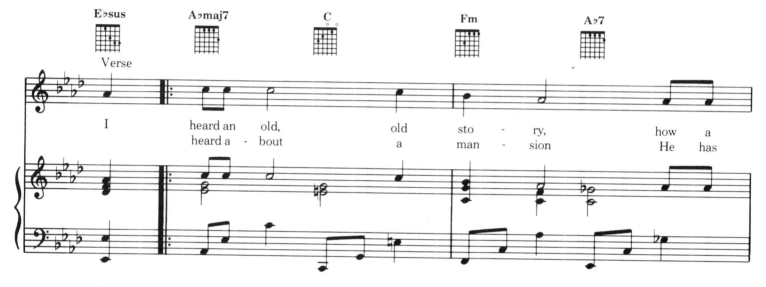

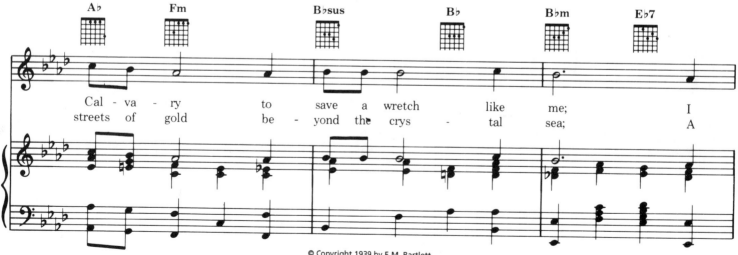

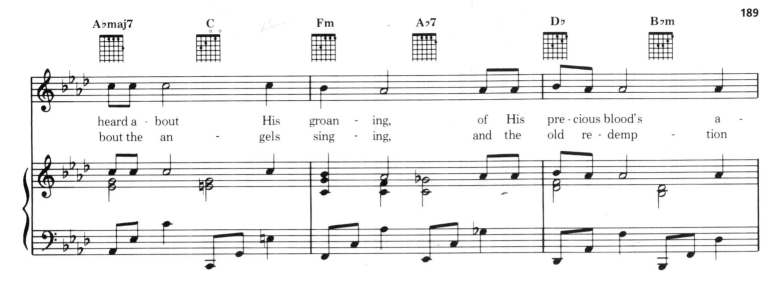

heard a - bout His groan - ing, of His pre - cious blood's a -
bout the an - gels sing - ing, and the old re - demp - tion

ton - ing, Then I re - pent - ed of my sins and
sto - ry, And some sweet day I'll sing up there the

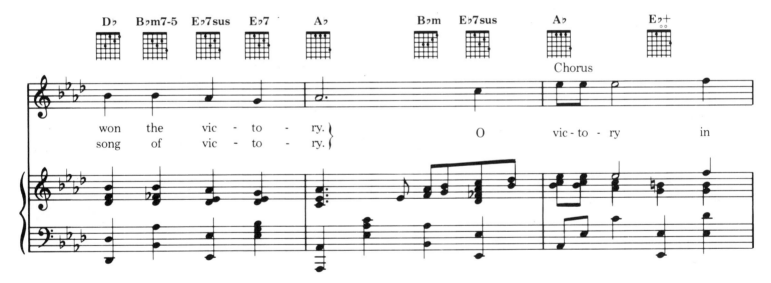

Chorus

won the vic - to - ry. } O vic - to - ry in
song of vic - to - ry. }

Je - sus, my Sav - ior, for - ev - er, He

190

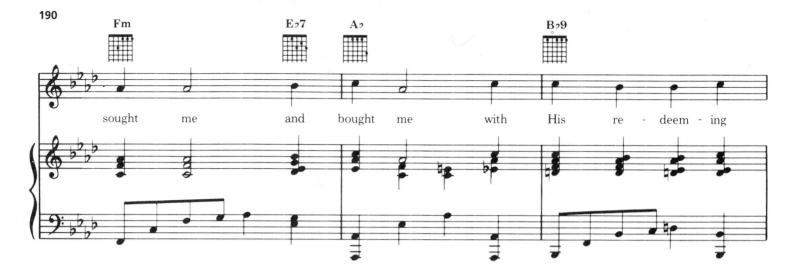

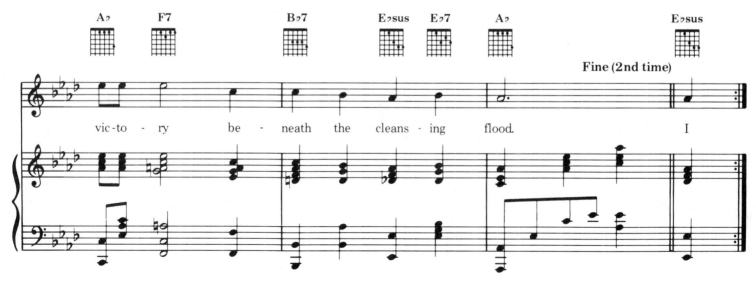

WHEN THE ROLL IS CALLED UP YONDER

Words and Music by
JAMES M. BLACK

WE SHALL BEHOLD HIM

Words and Music by
DOTTIE RAMBO

Majestically

The sky shall un -
an - gel shall

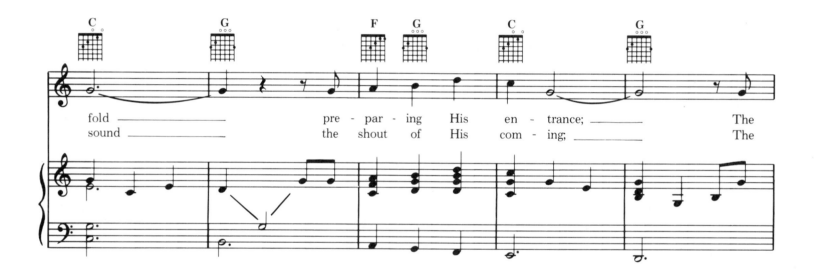

fold _____ pre - par - ing His en - trance; _____ The
sound _____ the shout of His com - ing; _____ The

stars will ap - plaud _____ Him _____ with thun - ders of
sleep - ing will rise _____ from their slum - ber - ing

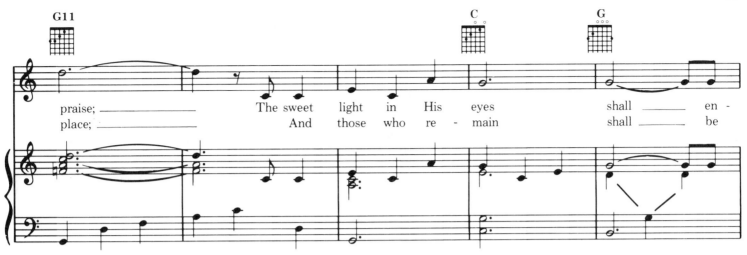
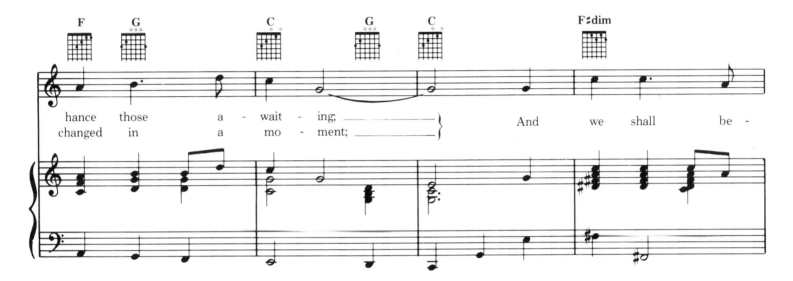
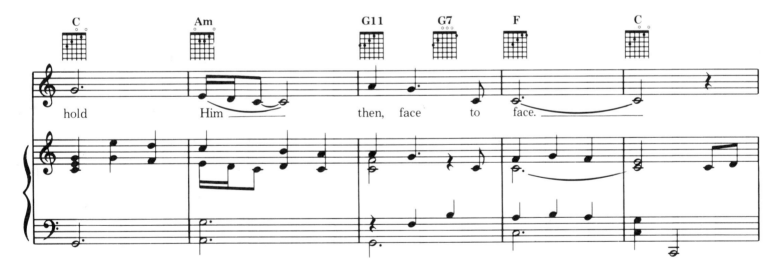
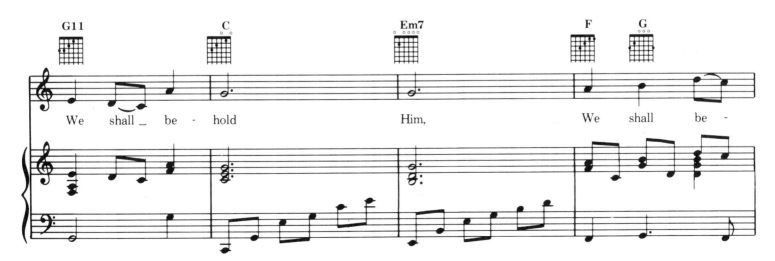

196

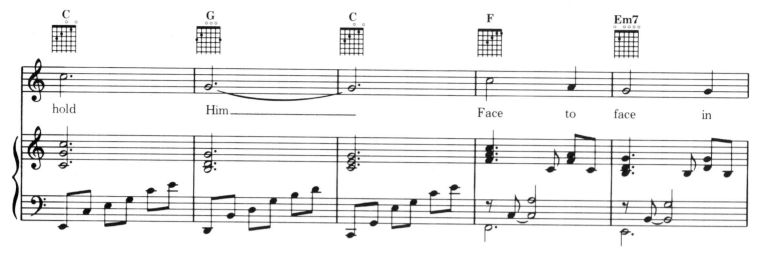

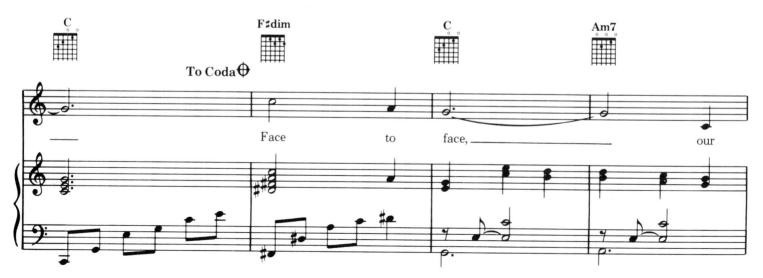

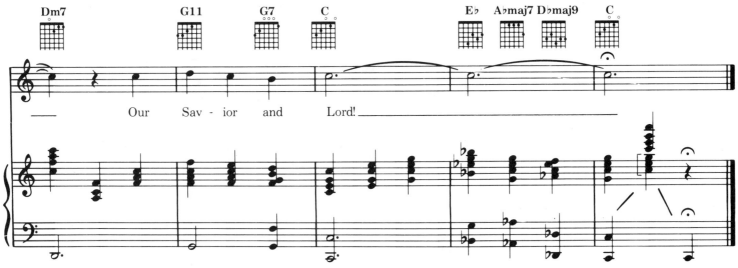

WE'LL UNDERSTAND IT BETTER BY AND BY

Words and Music by
CHARLES A. TINDLEY

1. We are of-ten tossed and driv-en on the
2.-4. *(See additional lyrics)*

rest-less sea of time, Som-ber skies and howl-ing tem-pests oft suc-ceed a bright sun-shine, In that

land of per-fect day, when the mists have rolled a-way, We will un-der-stand it bet-ter by and

Additional Lyrics

2. We are often destitute of the things that life demands,
   Want of food and want of shelter, thirsty hills and barren lands,
   We are trusting in the Lord, and according to His word,
   We will understand it better by and by.
   REFRAIN

3. Trials dark on every hand, and we cannot understand,
   All the ways that God would lead us to that blessed Promised Land;
   But He guides us with His eye and we'll follow till we die,
   For we'll understand it better by and by.
   REFRAIN

4. Temptations, hidden snares often take us unawares,
   And our hearts are made to bleed for a thoughtless word or deed,
   And we wonder why the test when we try to do our best,
   But we'll understand it better by and by.
   REFRAIN

WHISPERING HOPE

Words and Music by
ALICE HAWTHORNE

WHY ME?
(Why Me, Lord?)

Words and Music by
KRIS KRISTOFFERSON

Moderately, with a Gospel feeling

Why me, Lord? What have I ev-er done to de-serve e-ven
If you think there's a way I can try to re-

one of the plea-sures I've known? _____ Tell me, Lord, What did I ev-er
pay all I've ta-ken from you, _____ May be, Lord, I can show some-one

do that was worth lov-ing you, Or the kind-ness you've shown? _____
else what I've been thru my-self, On my way back to you. _____

WILL THE CIRCLE BE UNBROKEN

Words by ADA R. HABERSHON
Music by CHARLES H. GABRIEL

Moderately

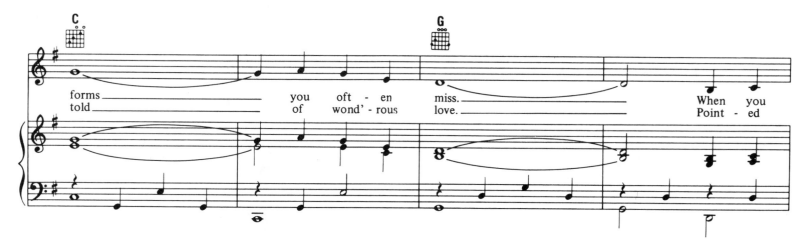

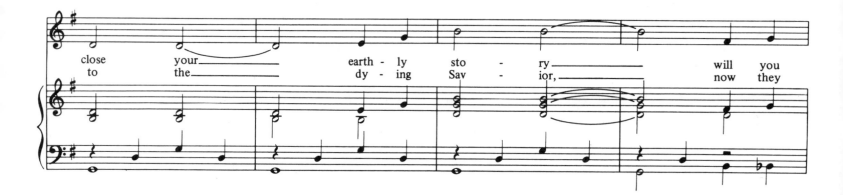

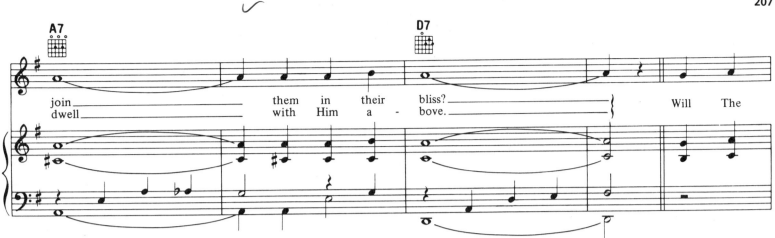

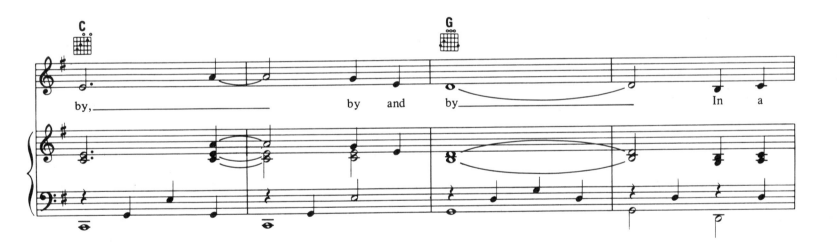

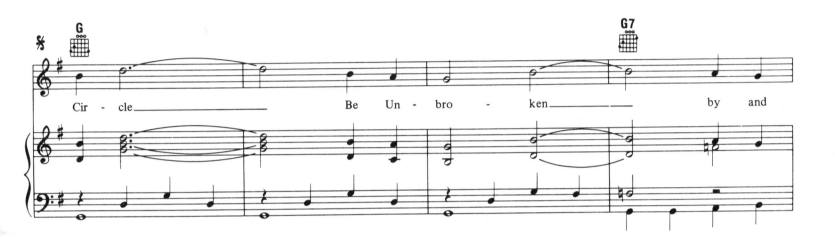

WINGS OF A DOVE

Words and Music by
BOB FERGUSON

When trou-bles sur-round us, _____ when
No-ah had drift - ed _____ on the

e - vils come, _____ The bod-y grows
flood man-y days, _____ He searched for

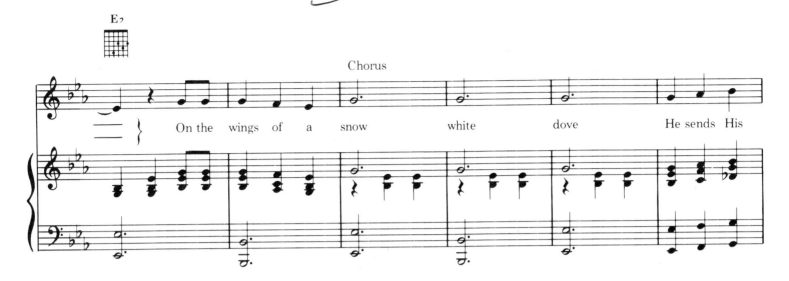

3. When Jesus went down to the waters that day,
   He was baptized in the usual way.
   When it was done, God blessed His Son.
   He sent him His love On the wings of a dove.

WRITTEN IN RED

Words and Music by
GORDON JENSEN

Warmly

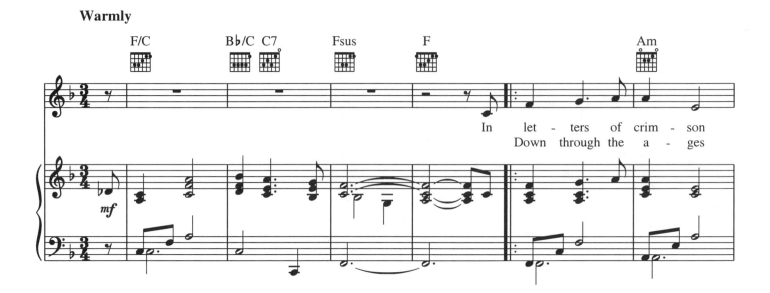

In let-ters of crim-son
Down through the a-ges

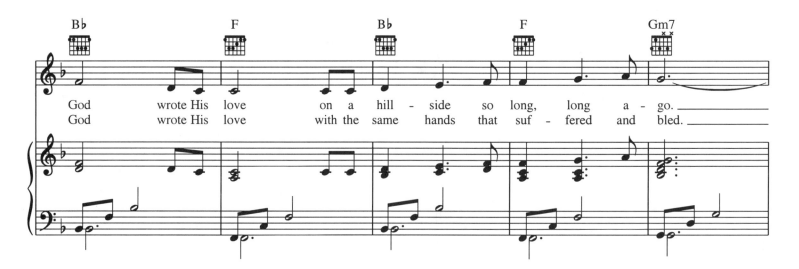

God wrote His love on a hill-side so long, long a-go.
God wrote His love with the same hands that suf-fered and bled.

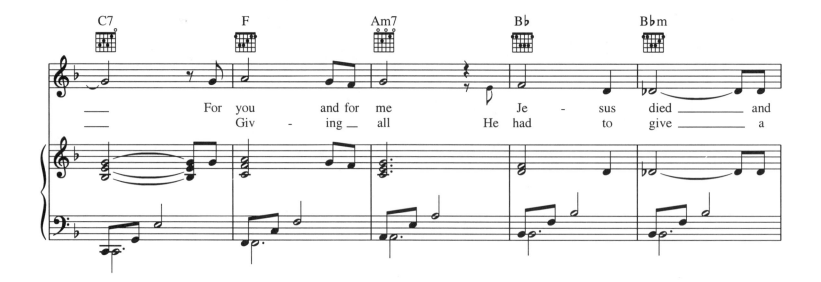

For you and for me Je-sus died and
Giv-ing all He had to give a

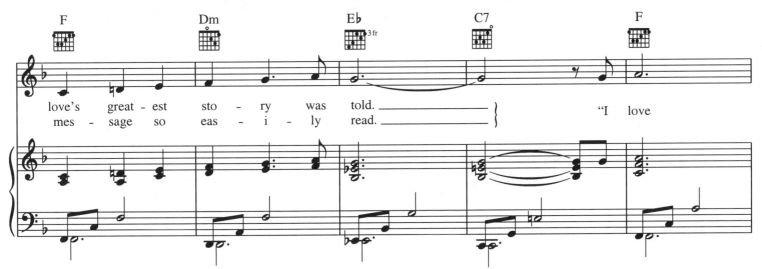

love's great - est sto - ry was told. _____ } "I love

mes - sage so eas - i - ly read. _____

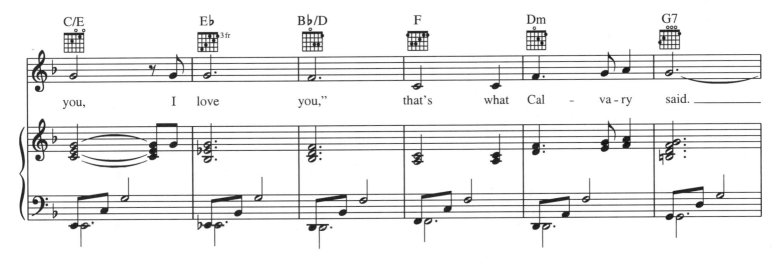

you, I love you," that's what Cal - va - ry said. _____

____ "I love you, I love _____ you, _____

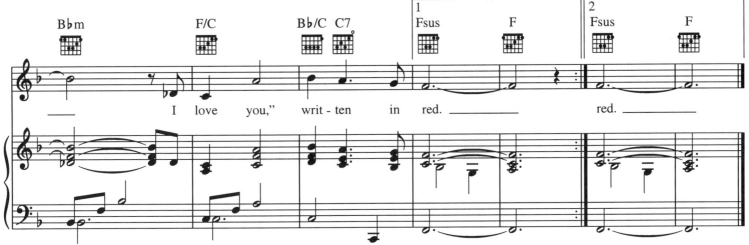

____ I love you," writ - ten in red. _____ red. _____

WONDERFUL GRACE OF JESUS

Traditional

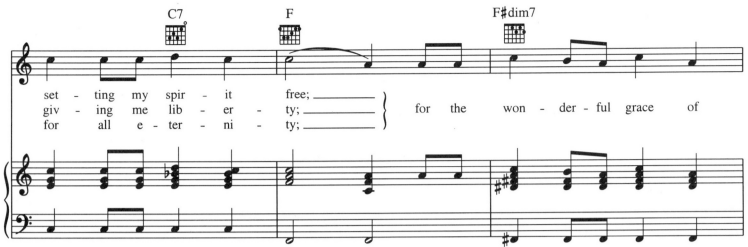

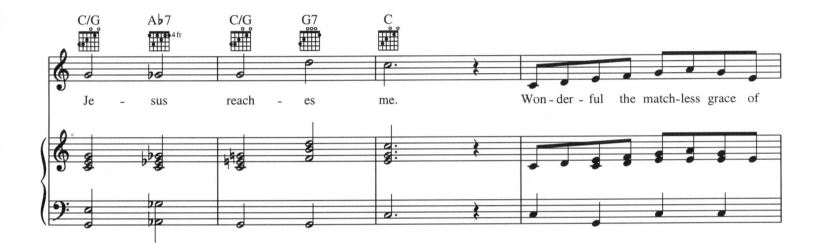

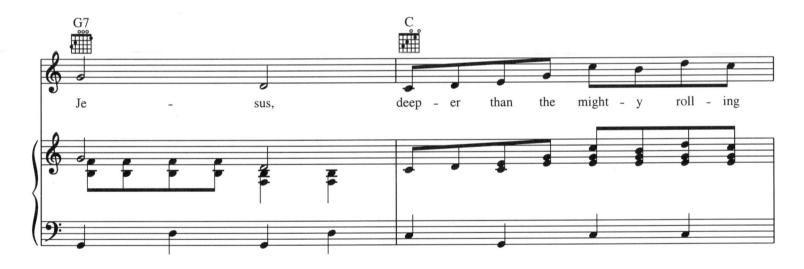

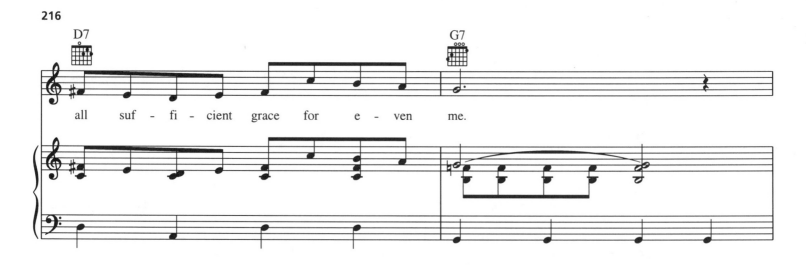

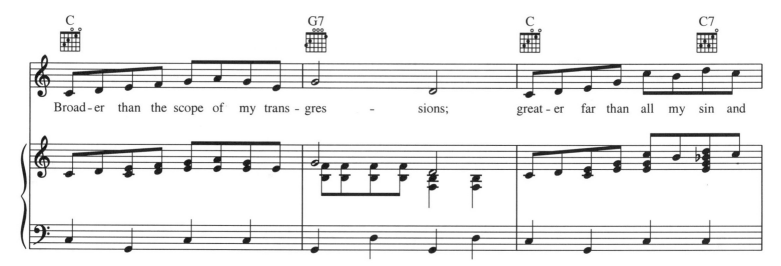

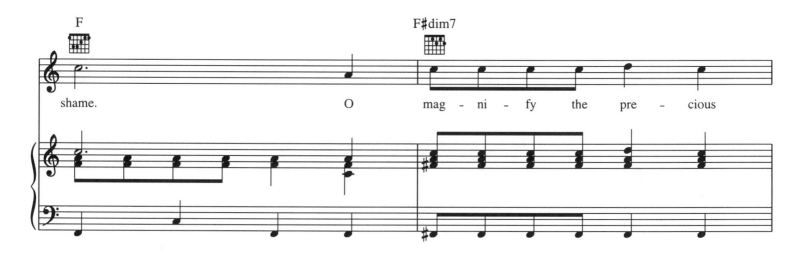

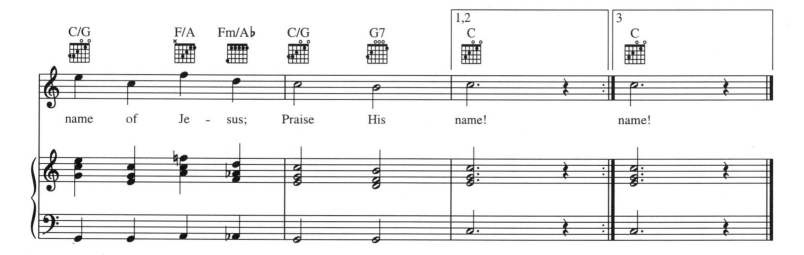